MAKING TOYS FOR PRESCHOOL CHILDREN

Using Ordinary Stuff for Extraordinary Play

Linda G. Miller
Mary Jo Gibbs

Illustrated by Kathy Dobbs

Dedication

From Mary Jo Gibbs

My personal thanks

To my friends--Rose, Angela, Janie, Sharon, Emily, Claire, Tami, Maria, Teri, and Jeanne--thanks for your support and encouragement! You are so special to me.

From Linda Miller

For creative teachers everywhere, and to those who (like me) like to see some directions. Happy teaching!

From Kathy Dobbs

For my husband Dale and son Sam—I love you both!

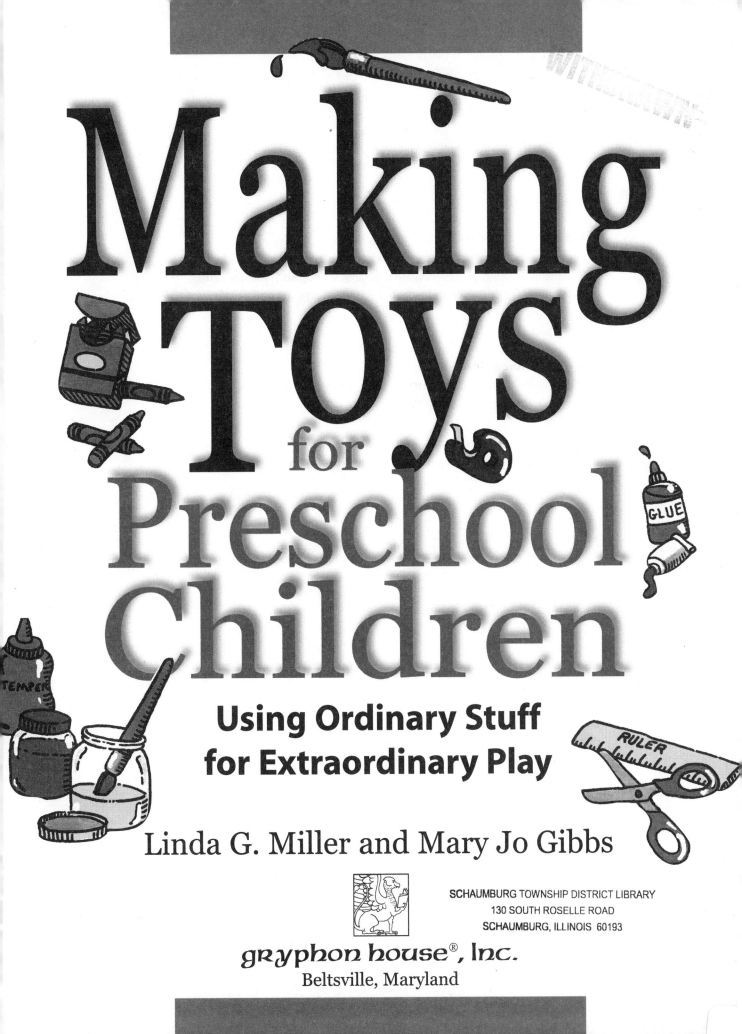

Making Toys for Preschool Children

for

Preschool Children

Using Ordinary Stuff for Extraordinary Play

Linda G. Miller and Mary Jo Gibbs

gryphon house®, Inc.
Beltsville, Maryland

Copyright

Illustrated by Kathy Dobbs

Library of Congress-Cataloging-in-Publication Data

Miller, Linda G.
  Making toys for preschool children : using ordinary stuff for extraordinary play / Linda G. Miller, Mary Jo Gibbs ; illustrated by Kathy Dobbs.
      p. cm.
Includes index.
  ISBN 0-87659-275-2
  1. Educational toys. 2. Educational games. 3. Education, Preschool--Activity programs. I. Gibbs, Mary Jo, 1946- II. Dobbs, Kathy. III. Title.
  LB1029.T6 M54 2002
  371.33'7--dc21

                                                    2002007413

Bulk purchase

Gryphon House books are available at special discount when purchased in bulk. Special editions or book excerpts also can be created to specification. For details, contact the Director of Sales at the address or phone number on this page.

Disclaimer

The publisher and the authors cannot be held responsible for injury, mishap, or damages incurred during the use of or because of the activities in this book. The authors recommend appropriate and reasonable supervision at all times based on the age and capability of each child.

Table of Contents

Introduction

Teachers of young children are some of the most creative individuals, but even they need fresh ideas occasionally. The activities and experiences presented in this book are simple and inexpensive, allowing you to spend your time having quality interactions with the children in your care. To determine which activities are appropriate for the children in your class, first observe to see where they are developmentally and what their interests are. Record your observations using anecdotal notes, so you will have a record of the children's progress.

Parents (and some teachers, too) often think that purchased toys are always superior to found or created items for young children. However, they might find that their young child prefers the box or even the wrapping paper to the gift that came in the box. Boxes are wonderful toys for stacking, carrying, nesting, filling, dumping, and matching. Children love climbing into and out of boxes, and very large boxes make great playhouses.

In addition, boxes and other simple materials are inexpensive "raw materials" for creating high-quality learning toys for young children. Toys also can be made from gloves, mittens, socks, pantyhose, and bags. Always begin with items that are completely empty and clean. The key to using found and discarded items as toys is being open to the limitless opportunities and the imagination of children. Think of the difference between a child playing with a toy phone that is always a phone and a box that can be a house, car, truck, train, step, and so on. It is the endless possibilities of these items that make them better than many purchased toys and a great way for a young child to learn.

Making Toys and Finding Materials

Making toys and finding interesting materials for young children to manipulate and play with do not need to be expensive or difficult tasks. Teachers often find that everyday household materials and teacher-made toys are by far the most interesting to children.

Be sure to consider the following guidelines for teacher-made toys:
- All gathered items (such as boxes, gloves, and so on) and materials (such as paint, glue, paper, and so on) that you use to transform

the items into toys must be non-toxic and safe in every way. Examine materials carefully, and read all labels.

- Make sure the toys encourage action and/or interaction rather than passive watching.
- If possible, make the toys responsive. If this is not possible, use them interactively.
- Make multiple toys. Share them with other teachers or put the extras aside until you need them.
- Work on making the toys multi-sensory, or make toys that have a variety of uses. That way you'll get more use out of the ones you do make.
- Check each homemade toy for safety. Check it again, and then ask another teacher to check it. Do not overlook safety issues. Always ask another adult to check the finished toy for safety. After you place it in the classroom, check it often to be certain that it remains safe for children.

Common household objects that are safe for children (even if the child decides to see how it tastes) are sometimes great toys. Begin with safe, clean materials. Ideas for toys that will enrich the play environment and that can be made from common objects include:

- **Simple Hand Puppets**—Made from socks, mittens, or even small boxes, puppets are a good way to capture a young child's attention.
- **Boxes**—All shapes and sizes of boxes are appropriate for building, stacking, nesting, and putting things in.
- **Sorting Toys**—A cardboard egg carton or a cupcake tin works well as a place to put objects (such as large spools, blocks, and cereal).
- **Dress-Ups**—Children enjoy putting on costumes, especially if there is a mirror, so that they can see themselves.
- **Blocks**—Use milk cartons of different sizes (half-pint, quart, half-gallon) to create blocks. Each block requires two cartons. Cut off the tops and put one carton bottom inside the other, so that the bottoms of the cartons make the ends of the block. Tape securely and cover with self-adhesive paper or paint.

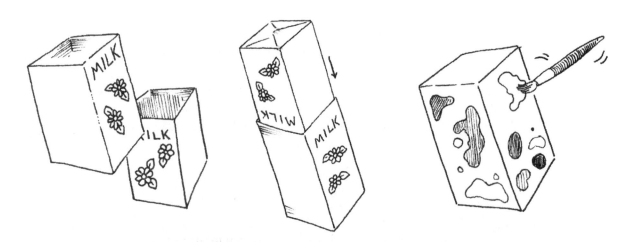

- **Books**—Use books throughout the classroom. Make a relatively "child-proof" book by cutting out large, bright, interesting pictures from magazines, pasting them on construction paper, covering both sides with clear contact paper, and putting the pages into a loose-leaf notebook.
- **Containers**—Plastic or metal (be sure edges are smooth) containers of all sizes and shapes can be used for stacking, nesting, and putting objects in, as well as in dramatic play.
- **Sorting Cans**—Cut the plastic lid of a coffee can, so that only certain shapes and sizes (blocks and spoons, for example) will fit through.

The beauty of teacher-made toys is that they are novel and interesting without costing much and can be discarded and replaced as they get used and worn out. New toys keep the environment interesting and fun for children. Create teacher-made toys in each developmental area. These toys can keep the job of planning fresh and give both the teacher and children new ways to create play together.

Experiences for Preschool Children

The ideas in this book support the traditional concept of interest areas. Plan for large blocks of time during the day when children can choose an area of interest and then play there long enough for complex play to emerge. Teachers often interact both with the child and with the new toy or situation (called triangulation). These interactions help children find interest in the novelty of the toy or situation, while feeling the security of having a familiar adult nearby.

Additionally, teachers must observe children to determine how to proceed, first to decide which activity or experience is the right one and then to determine if the child is receptive. If appropriate, do the activity with the child. Observe again to determine if you need to continue interacting with the child. Record your observations.

Activities in this book are included in the following interest areas:
Language Arts—Give children the opportunity to experiment with and learn about books both independently and interactively. Early experiences with books as sources of interesting images and stimulation form the foundation of literacy. Through experiences with books (both purchased and teacher-made), children learn emerging literacy skills such as:
- where to find the title, author, and illustrator;
- how to hold a book;
- where the book begins and ends;
- that words—not pictures—are read;
- that print goes from left to right and from the top to the bottom;

- that the beginning of a sentence sounds different from the end of the sentence; and
- that reading is a way to learn information.

When parents ask what they can do to help their children become good readers, tell them to read to their children each day and to set a great example as a reader of books.

Teachers should also make reading books a priority by reading to the children in the classroom every day. Parents will enjoy learning about the books you read to their children, so they can read the same or similar books at home. The rhyme and repetition in the language of songs, poems, rhymes, and fingerplays are important components of literacy development. Include many opportunities during the day to involve young children in this kind of interaction.

Provide enrichment opportunities by extending literacy experiences to the different interest areas in the classroom. Provide art materials so children can draw pictures about a story. Provide props so children can act out a story in dramatic play. Count items related to the story or put together related puzzles. All of these related activities reinforce language activities.

Creative Art—Art activities for young children are also sensory in nature. Very young children (unlike adults) may not care about how an art activity turns out. They are experiencing the moment—enjoying the feel of the fingerpaint, the smell of the crayons, the texture of the paper.

Avoid "cookie-cutter" art where all the projects appear the same. Instead, incorporate plenty of choices and time for children to develop their art experiences. When writing down what the child dictates about his or her picture, write the comments on a separate piece of paper or on the back. Do not damage the picture by writing on the face of it. Date all projects and write each child's name who participated.

Display art where children can see it at their own eye level. Save representative samples of art for children's portfolios.

Math and Manipulatives—Completing puzzles; sorting, grouping, and counting materials; creating patterns; and matching objects are all activities that will strengthen early math skills. Additionally, when children move around and manipulate items, they build skills in the area of math and manipulatives. Collect inexpensive materials, such as bottle caps, shells, stones, nuts inside their shells, pencils, and sticks, that will allow plenty of hands-on activities.

Dramatic Play—Provide a variety of simple, soft dolls representing a variety of ethnicities. They should be durable and washable, without eyes or parts that can come off with persistent handling. Young children need props like the ones they see in the real world, especially things associated with Mom or Dad (for example, purses, hats, bracelets, and keys). The teacher's role includes supplying play cues, participating with children as they play, and labeling what children do as they take on different roles. Dramatic play activities contribute to vocabulary development and to children's comprehension of the real world. In dramatic play, children are able to work through and understand issues that concern them or that they don't comprehend.

Blocks and Construction—Young children love to build things using blocks, boxes, sand, clay, and Star Links. However, these constructions often take time, sometimes more than one day. To give children more time to work on their constructions and to allow parents to view their children's work, label structures with a sign that says, "Building in progress by _____." Make clean-up time in the blocks and construction area a learning time by printing labels and pictures of items on the shelves where they are stored. In this way, cleaning up becomes a matching and sorting activity.

Science—Children are interested in their surroundings and in anything that they experience or imagine. Although many teachers are intimidated by science as a subject, children are ready to explore almost anything. Pets are a great way to introduce science into the classroom. Always check licensing standards before introducing any animal. As you explore different themes (such as farms, spring, and underwater), provide hands-on experiences, books, and music to reinforce them. Even an activity as simple as making mud is actually a hands-on science experience. Add interesting materials that allow children to explore textures, temperatures, light, and colors.

Sand and Water—Sand and water experiences, which are sensory in nature, are an essential part of education programs for young children. Water is soothing. Water toys stimulate play; the splashing and slapping of water produce interesting reactions. Put smaller tubs with only one or two inches of water inside small wading pools. Small wading pools make good dividers of activity space and make cleanup easier because spills are contained. Change the water and disinfect the container before another child uses it. These activities require very close supervision. A free-standing sand and water table can be used with a variety of materials, such as soil, colored water, packing pellets, or even gravel. Hide materials, such as animal figures, for children to find or include small vehicles and machinery for building roads.

Music and Movement—Preschool children enjoy exploring how their bodies move. A gym mat is a great place for these activities. Interact with children as you sing songs and do fingerplays. These experiences are opportunities for children to experiment with sounds, and they make wonderful transitions. If possible, provide a piece of climbing equipment and riding toys for use inside.

Outside—Outdoor time is an important part of the day for very young children. The fresh air is a welcome change from the closed environment of the classroom. The sounds of the neighborhood, the way light changes because of clouds or shade, and the feel of the breeze all add to the richness of the outdoor experience. Outdoor experiences also provide a change of pace and variety for the teacher. The teacher's role is interactive, inviting children to learn as they explore. Additionally, activities that are moved from the inside to the outside take on a new meaning.

How to Use This Book

This book includes activities for the following interest areas:

- Language Arts
- Creative Art
- Math and Manipulatives
- Dramatic Play
- Blocks and Construction
- Science
- Sand and Water
- Music and Movement
- Outside

Use this book in many ways, including:
- Select an inexpensive material such as bags, boxes, socks, or gloves and then scan the book or use the index to choose activities according to the materials that are available.
- Choose activities based solely on the interest areas of the book.
- Provide a well-rounded, developmentally appropriate classroom for young children by selecting activities from each of the nine sections throughout the book.
- Use the book to get fresh ideas for a theme-based curriculum. Activities fit a wide variety of themes.

Interpreting Each Activity

Each activity has:

Material Icon—shows the main material needed to create the toy.

Materials List—includes all essential materials needed to complete the activity. Materials are generally common arts and crafts supplies that are familiar and easily accessible to teachers. Every effort has been made to use materials that are free, recycled, or very inexpensive. Always keep in mind safety precautions when using any materials, and especially if you substitute materials other than those listed. Closely supervise children, so they do not put dangerous items (such as plastic bags) into their mouths.

To Make—provides step-by-step instructions for creating the toy. Many activities are illustrated to make the process even easier. As much as possible, involve the children in making the toys. It is always advisable to try the activity before presenting it to a child or involving a child in the activity. Think about safety and be aware of tools or materials used by an adult that are not intended for small children. Often teachers will be directed to use tools away from the children.

To Use—suggests ways that a child or children can use the activity; however, teachers and children may very well find their own ways to enjoy the activities. Follow all safety precautions, and supervise children closely at all times.

Language Arts

Fun Packs

 Bags

Materials
child-sized tote bags
storybooks
writing paper
crayons and pencils

To Make
- Place a storybook, paper, pencils, and crayons inside each tote bag.

To Use
- Children use the tote bag as a portable reading/writing center at school or take it home to share reading and writing with their parents.

"All About Me" Bags

Bags

Materials
brown paper grocery bags
art materials, including glue and markers

To Make
- Give each child a grocery bag and help him print his name on it.
- Encourage the children to use art supplies to decorate their bag.

To Use
- Each child takes his bag home and fills it with a few items to share for "show and tell."
- At circle time each day, ask two or three children to share their "All About Me" Bag with the group.

Restaurant Bag Book

 Bags

Materials
fast food restaurant bags
hole punch
yarn

To Make
- Collect a variety of familiar fast food restaurant bags.
- Punch holes into the sides of the bags and fasten them together with pieces of yarn to make a book.

To Use
- Children "read" the book alone or with a friend.

Grocery Bag Journals

 Bags

Materials
brown paper grocery bags
scissors
hole punch
yarn
crayons, markers, and pencils

To Make
- Cut out the fronts and backs of grocery bags.
- Punch holes into the sides of the bags. Fasten the pages together with yarn.

To Use
- Children use crayons, markers, and pencils to write on the pages.
- Add more pages as the journal progresses.
- Children can also use these books to draw pictures on the pages and write or dictate stories to go with the pictures.

Grocery Bag Big Books

Bags

Materials

paper grocery bags
hole punch
silver book rings
storybook
crayons, markers, or collage materials

To Make

- Stack several paper grocery bags on top of each other. Punch holes into the left side of the grocery bags about 1" from the fold.
- Fasten them together with silver book rings.

To Use

- Read a storybook to the children.
- Ask the children to retell the story. As they do, write their words on a page of the grocery bag book.
- Children use crayons, markers, or collage materials to illustrate the pages.

Baggie Books

 Bags

Materials

construction paper
scissors
resealable plastic bags
photos or magazine pictures
glue
hole punch
ribbon or yarn

To Make

- Cut construction paper to fit inside the resealable bags.
- Glue photos or magazine pictures onto the construction paper pieces. Insert each picture into a resealable plastic bag and seal it.
- Put several bags together, punch holes into the "zippered" side of the bags, and fasten them together with ribbon or yarn.

To Use

- Children "read" the book.

Lunch Bag Book

 Bags

Materials

paper lunch bags
animal pictures
scissors
glue
markers
hole punch
brad fasteners

To Make

- Fold the bottoms of about four or five lunch bags over to one side.
- If necessary, cut animal pictures to fit on the bags.
- Glue an animal picture onto each bag, so that part of the picture is hidden underneath the flap.

- Use markers to label each picture.
- Punch holes in the open ends of the bags and then secure the pages together with brad fasteners.

To Use

- Children guess what the animal is, then open the flap to see the whole picture.

Lunch Bag Puppets

Bags

Materials

brown paper lunch bags
newspapers
glue
craft sticks
yarn
art supplies

To Make

- Stuff the paper bag with crumpled newspapers.
- Place glue on a craft stick and stick it inside the opening of the bag.
- Tie the opening securely closed with yarn.
- Turn the bag upside down and use art materials to create a face, hair, and decorations to hide the tied opening.

To Use

- Children use the bag puppets to act out stories.

Black Cat Bag Puppet

Bags

Materials

brown paper lunch bags
black paint
paintbrush
glue
craft sticks
white chalk
black construction paper
scissors
gray or white yarn

To Make

- Paint a lunch bag using black paint.
- Place a glue-covered craft stick inside the opening of the bag and secure it with yarn.
- When the paint is dry, draw a cat's face using white chalk on the bottom of the bag.
- Cut out ears from black construction paper and glue them into place on the bag.
- Glue on strands of white or gray yarn for whiskers.

To Use

- Children use the cat puppet to tell stories or sing songs.
- Use a tape recorder to document what children are doing. Observe how they use the puppet and write an anecdotal note.

Paper Bag Character Hats

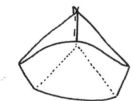 **Bags**

Materials

large, brown paper bags
scissors
stapler or tape
markers
loop and hook fasteners, such as Velcro

To Make

- Cut off the bottom of the bag and cut the bag on the seam side so that it lays flat.
- Fold the bag to make a three-point hat or cut as shown in the illustration.
- Staple or tape the hat to secure it in place.
- Use other flattened bags to draw story, nursery rhyme, or fingerplay characters. Cut them out.
- Attach loop and hook fasteners (Velcro) onto the front of the hats and onto the backs of the character pieces.

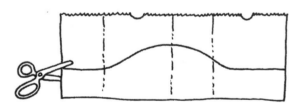

To Use

- Children wear the hats and place the character pieces onto their hats when acting out a story, nursery rhyme, or fingerplay.

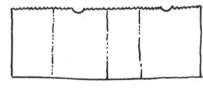

Monkey Masks

Bags

Materials

large, brown paper grocery bags
scissors
markers

To Make

- Measure about 12" from the bottom of the bag.
- Cut the bag as shown in the illustration. Use the bag bottoms to make the monkeys.
- Cut out an oval the size of a child's face on one wide side of the bag.
- Use markers to draw the monkey's head (no face) with ears around the hole.

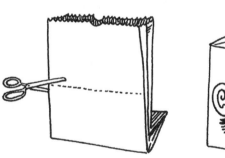  

To Use

- Children place the bags over their heads and peep through the oval to be a monkey.
- The masks are fun to wear while acting out monkey songs.

Character Smocks

Bags

Materials

large, brown paper bags

scissors

markers, paint and paintbrushes, or other art materials

To Make

- Cut out the narrow sides of the bag, leaving the wide sides and the bottom intact.
- Lay the flattened paper on the table. Cut out a hole large enough for a child's head to fit through in the reinforced bottom of the bag.
- Use markers, paint, or other art materials to create characters on the wide panels of the bags.

remove narrow sides...

cut a hole to fit a child's head

To Use

- Children put their heads through the hole and wear the remaining sides of the bag in the front and back of their bodies.
- Character Smocks are fun for role-playing favorite stories and songs.

Puppet Stage

Bags

Materials

large paper grocery bag
markers or crayons
construction paper
glue or tape
scissors
craft sticks

To Make

- Choose a favorite fingerplay or rhyme and draw a background for it onto one wide side of the bag. Or you can glue on construction paper scenery, if desired.
- Draw or trace fingerplay characters onto construction paper. Cut them out and glue or tape them onto craft sticks.
- Cut slits into the background scenery big enough to slide the craft stick characters into appropriate places on the background.
- Cut out a large circle in the wide part of the back of the bag.

cut slits in the bag to allow for movement of characters....

To Use

- Hold the bag in your lap with one hand inside the hole in the back of the bag to move the stick puppets.
- Repeat the fingerplay or rhyme and as you do, push each character stick through the slits to act out the fingerplay or rhyme.

"I Am Thankful" Turkey

 Bags

Materials

2 large, brown grocery bags
newspapers
rubber band
construction paper
scissors
tape
markers
craft sticks

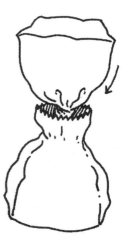

To Make

- Stuff one bag with crumpled newspapers until it is full.
- Fill the other bag with crumpled newspapers until the bag can be shaped into a "head."
- Place the head into the opening of the first bag and gather the opening around the head.
- Use a rubber band to attach the head onto the bag body.
- Cut out eyes, a beak, a wattle, and feet from construction paper.
- Tape the turkey features onto the bag.
- Cut out a variety of colored construction paper feathers.

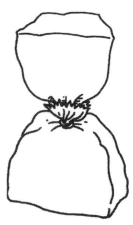

To Use

- Children write or dictate "I am thankful" messages onto the feathers.
- Tape a craft stick onto the backs of the feathers and push the sticks into the bag to form wings and tail feathers.

Skunk Hole Game

Bags

Materials

large, brown grocery bag
scissors
green tissue paper
rubber band
pictures of skunks
pictures of animals, shapes, colors, foods, and so on

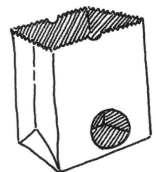

To Make

- Cut out a hole near the bottom of one wide side of the bag. The hole needs to be large enough for a child's hand to fit through easily.
- Gather the opening of the bag together and wrap a sheet of green tissue paper around the twisted bag opening.
- Use a rubber band to secure the opening closed.

- Use scissors to cut the tissue paper into strips for grass.
- Place pictures of your choice (animals, shapes, colors, foods, and so on) and several pictures of skunks inside the bag opening.

twist up the top

To Use

- Gather the children into a circle. Pass the "Skunk's Hole" around the circle.
- Each child removes a picture and identifies what it is.
- When a child pulls out a skunk picture, everybody stands and says, "Pew-w-w-w!"
- The following chant is an exaggerated, funny way of telling the story and can be used with the game.

secure tissue paper with rubber band

"Little Skunk's Hole"

Well, I stuck my hand in a little skunk hole,
And the little skunk said, "Well, bless my soul!
Take it out. Take it out. Remove it!"
Well, I didn't take it out, and the little skunk said,
"You'd better take it out, or you'll wish you had.
Take it out. Take it out. Remove it!"
Well, I didn't take it out, and the little skunk said. "Psssssssssst,"
And I removed it!

Story Box

 Boxes

Materials

small box
small objects (such as toy cars, small dolls, toy furniture, or plastic animals)

To Make

- Place the small objects inside the box.

To Use

- Pass the box around to each child.
- As each child removes an object, incorporate the object into a group story.
- Write the story on chart paper so it can be shared again.

Box Front Book

 Boxes

Materials
food boxes (such as cereal, snack food, macaroni and cheese, and
  so on)
scissors
hole punch
yarn

To Make
- Cut off the fronts of the different food boxes.
- Punch holes into the left side of each box front, one at the top
  and one at the bottom.
- Thread pieces of yarn through the holes to fasten the pages
  together.

To Use
- Children are familiar with the food boxes, so they can "read" this
  book.

Story Cube

 Boxes

Materials
cube-shaped facial tissue box
newspaper
tape
magazine pictures of various objects, people, and animals
scissors
glue
clear contact paper

To Make

- Stuff the tissue box with newspaper and tape it securely closed.
- Cut out pictures from magazines.
- Cut the pictures to fit on the tissue box and glue a picture to each side of the box.
- Cover the box with clear contact paper.

To Use

- Take turns rolling the cube on the floor.
- Ask one child to name the picture that lands on top.
- Incorporate the picture into a group story.
- Write the story onto chart paper as new information is added.

Roly-Poly Portraits

 Boxes

Materials

2 half-pint wax milk cartons per 6 children
craft knife (adults only)
old newspapers
tape
photos of children
glue
sticky label
fine-tip marker or pen

To Make

- Away from the children, use a craft knife to cut off the tops of the milk cartons. You will need two milk cartons per six children in the class.
- Place crumpled newspaper inside one of the carton halves.
- Turn the other carton half upside down and fit the stuffed milk carton into it.
- Secure the cartons together with tape.
- Glue photos of the children on each of the six sides, so that each side has a photo of one child on it.
- Make enough carton blocks so that each child's picture is on one side of a block.
- Print each child's name on a sticky label to match with the child's photo. Place the sticky label underneath the photo.

cut tops off the cartons...

stuff with paper...

secure with tape...

Kevin

Cassandra

To Use
■ Use the Roly-Poly Portraits for name recognition, to assign jobs, or for playing games.

Rolling Rhymes

 Boxes

Materials
cube-shaped facial tissue box
newspaper
construction paper
scissors
glue
fine-tip markers
clear contact paper

To Make

- Stuff the tissue box with newspaper.
- Cut construction paper to fit around the tissue box.
- Cover the tissue box with construction paper and glue it in place.
- Print the words to a different nursery rhyme on each side of the box.
- On each side, also draw a picture that describes the nursery rhyme.
- Cover the box with clear contact paper.

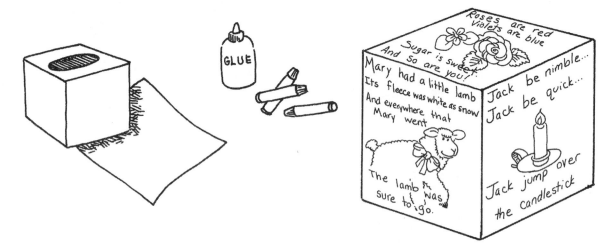

To Use

- Read the rhymes with the children.
- Roll the box to choose which rhyme to read next.

Box Book

Boxes

Materials

aluminum foil or wax paper box with an empty cardboard tube inside

colorful contact paper

shelf-lining paper (without adhesive)

markers

tape

To Make

- Remove the sharp tear strip from the box.
- Cover the box with colorful contact paper.
- Draw pictures and write the text of a familiar story on shelf-lining paper.
- Tape the end of the shelf liner story to the cardboard tube and roll the story around the tube.
- Place the tube inside the decorated box and label the box with the name of the story.

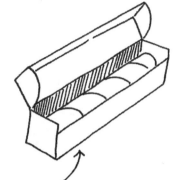

remove
sharp "teeth"
from box...

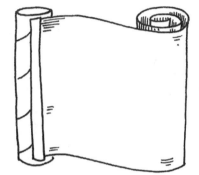

attach shelf paper
with tape...

To Use

- As you read the story, pull the paper from the box.
- After reading the story, roll the story back onto the tube and store inside the box.
- Make several "Box Books." Keep them where the children can choose their own story and "read" it on their own.

Story Box

 Boxes

Materials
shoebox with lid
felt
scissors
greeting cards or cereal boxes
glue

To Make
- Cut a piece of felt to fit inside the lid of the shoebox and glue it in place.
- Cut out characters from greeting cards or from the fronts and backs of cereal boxes.
- Glue small pieces of felt onto the backs of the cut-out characters.
- Put the pictures inside the box and put the lid on.
- Store the pictures inside the box.

To Use
- Children stick the characters on the felt on the lid to create stories.

Cereal Box Flannel Board

 Boxes

Materials
cereal box
newspapers
tape
felt
scissors
glue
flannel board figures

To Make

- Stuff the cereal box with crumpled newspapers.
- Tape the opening securely closed.
- Cover the entire box with felt and glue it in place.
- Cut out a rectangle from a piece of felt that is a different color than the felt covering the box.
- Glue three sides of the rectangle onto one side of the box to make a pocket.
- Place flannel board figures inside the pocket.

To Use

- Children place the characters on the felt board as you tell a story or use the felt characters to tell their own story.

Tissue Box Puppets

 Boxes

Materials

cube-shaped facial tissue box
art supplies
tape or glue
empty paper towel roll

To Make

- Turn the tissue box upside down and use art materials to decorate it to resemble an animal or person.
- Place an empty paper towel tube into the opening of the tissue box and secure it with glue or tape.

To Use

- Hold onto the cardboard tube and use the puppet to tell stories with children.

Salt Box Puppet

 Boxes

Materials

pencil
toilet tissue tube
cylinder-shaped salt box
craft knife (adults only)
tape
construction paper
scissors
glue
yarn

push into hole and secure with tape...

SALT

To Make

- Trace around the toilet tissue tube on one end of the salt box.
- Away from the children, use a craft knife to cut out the circle created by tracing the toilet tissue tube. Push the tissue tube into the hole, and secure it with tape.
- Cover the salt box with construction paper and glue it in place.
- Cut out facial features from construction paper and glue them into place.
- Glue yarn on top for hair.

To Use

- Children hold the tube to make the puppet move as they tell a story.

Hamburger Box Puppet

 Boxes

Materials
craft knife (adults only)
fast food hamburger box (Styrofoam)
plastic wiggle eyes
glue
marker

To Make
- Away from the children, use a craft knife to cut off the fastener tabs on the box.
- Glue two wiggle eyes on the upper potion of the front part of the box.
- Use a marker to draw a mouth on the lower portion of the front part of the box.
- Carefully cut out a hole in the top and the lower part of the back of the box (see illustration).

remove the fastener tabs...

glue on mouth and→ eyes...

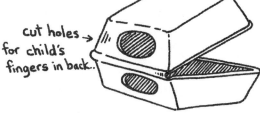

cut holes → for child's fingers in back...

To Use
- Children put their fingers into the holes in the back of the box and wiggle them to make the puppet's mouth open and close.
- The puppet may be a part of a story or song.

Matchbox Puppets

 Boxes

Materials

art supplies

glue

small and large empty matchboxes (sliding type)

red construction paper

scissors

craft sticks

tape

To Make

- Use art supplies and glue to make a face on a wide side of the matchbox.
- Cut out a piece of red construction paper to fit into the bottom of the drawer part of the box. Glue it in place.
- Cut out a slot in the drawer part of the matchbox. Tape a craft stick through the slot.

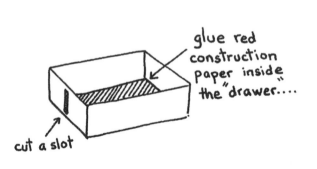
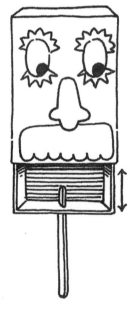

cut a slot

glue red construction paper inside the "drawer"....

To Use

- Children use the puppet to act out stories.
- They use the craft stick to open and close the puppet's mouth.

Cereal Box Puppet Pal

 Boxes

Materials

large cereal box
white or beige craft paper
tape
craft knife (adults only)
2 toilet tissue tubes
scissors
construction paper
glue
yarn

To Make

- Remove the lid from the cereal box and turn it upside down.
- Cover the box with craft paper and tape it in place.
- Away from the children, use a craft knife to cut out a hole into both narrow sides of the box. Then push a cardboard tube into each hole to make arms.
- Cut out two hands from construction paper and glue them onto the ends of the tubes.
- Cut out construction paper facial features and glue them into place.
- Glue yarn onto the top and sides of the box for hair.

To Use

- Children place a hand inside the box to make the puppet act out a story.

Cereal Box Buddy

 Boxes

Materials
cereal box
newspapers
tape
tempera paint
paintbrushes
construction paper
scissors
glue
yarn
paper plate

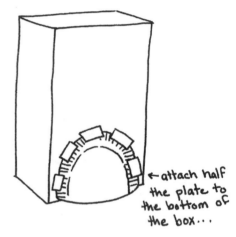

To Make

- Stuff the cereal box with crumpled newspapers and seal it closed with tape.
- Paint the box with tempera paint and allow it to dry.
- Cut out facial features from construction paper and glue them into place on the box.
- Glue yarn for hair on top of the box.
- Cut a paper plate in half.
- Tape one half of the paper plate onto the back of the box, so the straight side of the plate is at the bottom. Leave the straight side un-taped.

← attach half the plate to the bottom of the box...

To Use

- Place a hand under the paper plate half on the back of the box to move the puppet while telling a story.

Cereal Box Blue Birdie

 Boxes

Materials

cereal box
newspapers
blue tempera paint
paintbrushes
2 shoulder pads
orange tempera paint
craft knife (adults only)
glue
buttons
craft feathers
paper towel tube

To Make

- Stuff the cereal box with crumpled newspaper.
- Paint the cereal box blue and allow it to dry.
- Paint the shoulder pads orange and allow them to dry.
- Away from the children, use a craft knife to cut a slit into the center of one wide side of the box.
- Turn the box so that the bottom becomes the top.
- Place the shoulder pads together to form a beak and push them through the slit in the box. Glue the beak into place.
- Glue button "eyes" in place.
- Glue a few colorful feathers on the top of the box.
- Push a paper towel tube inside the box opening and secure with tape.

To Use

- Children hold the paper towel tube to control the puppet as they tell a story or sing a song.

Tissue Box Stage

 Boxes

Materials

rectangular facial tissue box
craft knife (adults only)
stickers or small pictures
tape
craft sticks

To Make

- Turn the tissue box on its side.
- Away from the children, use a craft knife to cut off the side of the box that is now facing up (see illustration).
- Hold the box so that the cut-out side is at the bottom and the tissue opening is facing forward.
- Tape stickers or small pictures to craft sticks to make puppets. Or use finger puppets if available.

remove shaded side...

To Use

- Children use the puppet stage and puppets to act out stories.
- They hold the box with one hand and put the finger puppets or stick puppets in the other hand. Then they place the hand holding the puppets inside the bottom of the box, so the puppets are visible through the tissue opening on the front side.

Theme-Related Puppet Houses

 Boxes

Materials

large cardboard box
paint
paintbrushes
craft knife (adults only)
variety of puppets

To Make

- Paint a cardboard box to resemble a barn, house, or any other theme-related building.
- Away from the children, use a craft knife to cut out doors and windows in the box for puppets to hang out of.

To Use

- Children use puppets with the building to act out stories.

Box Tree

 Boxes

Materials

3 cube-shaped cardboard boxes of graduated sizes
masking tape
craft knife (adults only)
long cardboard tubes
brown and black paint
paintbrushes
scissors
colored construction paper
glue
puppets

← tape boxes together

To Make

- Stack the three boxes on top of each other, with the largest on the bottom and the smallest on top.
- Tape the boxes together with masking tape.
- Away from the children, use a craft knife to cut out oval-shaped holes into one side of each box.
- Cut out more holes on the other sides of each box. Push cardboard tubes into the holes, leaving a long portion of each tube sticking out.
- Paint the boxes and tubes with brown paint.
- When the brown paint is dry, use black paint to make wood grain marks to define the tree trunk and limbs.
- Cut out colorful construction paper leaves and glue them onto the cardboard tube "tree limbs."
- Place animal puppets into the oval holes in the tree or sitting on the limbs.

To Use

- Children play with the puppets in the "tree."

Jack-in-the-Box

 Boxes

Materials

dryer vent hose
scissors
oatmeal container
heavy tape
felt scraps
glue
construction paper
markers

To Make

- Cut a piece of dryer vent hose twice as long as the oatmeal container.
- Cover any wire ends with heavy tape.
- Cut out a felt circle a little bigger than the end of the dryer hose. Tape it securely to one end of the dryer hose.
- Cut out clown facial features from felt scraps and glue them onto the felt circle at the end of the dryer hose to make a face.
- Decorate the oatmeal container with construction paper and markers.
- Push the "Jack" puppet (the hose) down into the container and place the lid on top. When the top is opened, Jack will spring out of the box.

glue a felt face on one end of the hose.....

To Use

- Children push the puppet inside, remove the top, and enjoy the excitement of "Jack" popping out.

Walkie-Talkies

 Boxes

Materials

small, rectangular box with lid (jewelry box)
glue
aluminum foil
markers
2 milk jug lids
drinking straw

To Make

- Glue the box lid onto the box.
- Cover the box with aluminum foil and glue it in place.
- Use a marker to draw dots in a concentric circle pattern in the center of one end of the box.
- Glue two milk jug tops for knobs on the opposite end of the box (see illustration).
- Cover a drinking straw with aluminum foil and glue it to one long side of the box for an antenna.

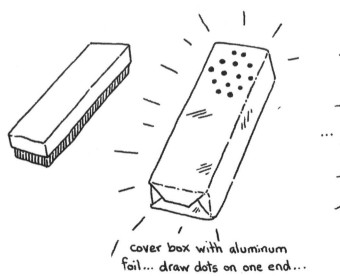

cover box with aluminum foil... draw dots on one end...

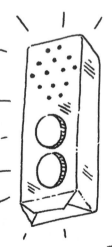

glue on milk jug tops...

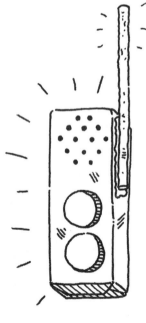

glue on foil-covered drinking straw...

To Use

- Children talk with friends across the room or playground using the walkie-talkies.
- Make several, so children can use them to communicate with each other as they role-play.

Storytelling Glove

 Gloves/Mittens

Materials
pictures of story characters
pen or marker
felt
scissors
cotton glove
hook and loop fasteners, such as Velcro

To Make
- Trace pictures of story characters on a piece of felt and cut them out. (Coloring books offer great patterns.) Or use commercial flannel board characters.
- Attach hook and loop fasteners (Velcro) to the backs of the felt characters and to the glove.

To Use
- Wear the glove and attach the characters to it while reading or telling a story.

Stuffed Glove

 Gloves/Mittens

Materials
cotton gloves
fiberfill
needle and thread
non-toxic permanent markers

To Make
- Stuff the glove with fiberfill.
- Sew the opening securely closed.
- Use permanent markers to draw facial features on the palm of the glove.

To Use
- Use the puppet to act out stories or to sing songs.

Glove and Plate Puppets

 Gloves/Mittens

Materials

gloves
glue
sturdy paper plates
art supplies

To Make

- Glue a glove onto the back of each sturdy paper plate.
- Use art supplies to decorate the paper plates to make people faces, animal faces, or fantasy creatures.

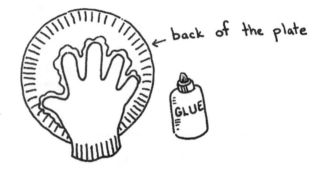

← back of the plate

To Use

- Children place a hand inside the glove and manipulate the puppet to act out a story or song.

Mitten Rabbit

 Gloves/Mittens

Materials
white, black, and pink felt
scissors
glue or needle and thread
mitten
pink pompom

To Make
- Cut out rabbit ears from white felt. Glue or sew them onto the back of the hand part of the mitten.
- Cut out eyes from black felt and glue or sew them onto the mitten.
- Glue or sew a pink pompom in place to make a nose.

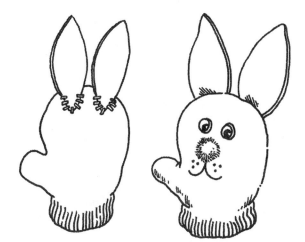

To Use
- Put the Mitten Rabbit on your hand and use it to sing a song or tell a story.

Bunny Mitt

 Gloves/Mittens

Materials
white craft foam
scissors
wiggle eyes
tiny pink pompoms
white fabric glove
hot glue gun (adults only)

To Make

- Cut out five sets of two tiny bunny ears from white craft foam.
- Away from the children, use the hot glue gun to attach the ears on the fingertips of a white fabric glove. Glue two ears to each fingertip.
- Then use the hot glue gun to attach two wiggle eyes onto each fingertip and two tiny pink pompoms under each set of eyes.

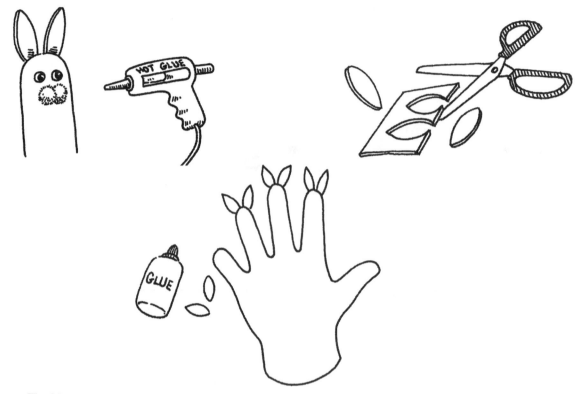

To Use

- Use the Bunny Mitts to sing songs such as "Little Bunny, Foo Foo"; to act out fingerplays such as "Here Is a Bunny"; or to tell bunny stories, such as "The Hare and the Tortoise."

Mouse Finger Puppet

 Gloves/Mittens

Materials
old glove
scissors
felt scraps
glue
yarn

To Make
- Cut off a finger from the glove.
- Cut out ears, eyes, and a nose from felt scraps. Glue them into place on the cut-out fingertip.
- Glue a short length of yarn at the bottom of the fingertip for a tail.

To Use
- Place the Mouse Finger Puppet on a finger and move it to make it "talk."

Caterpillar to Butterfly Puppets

 Gloves/Mittens

Materials
old glove
scissors
green and black pompoms
glue
wiggle eyes
felt scraps
cotton ball

To Make

- Cut off a finger from the glove.
- Glue a green pompom on the tip of the cut-out finger.
- Glue wiggle eyes onto the pompom to make a caterpillar.
- Cut off a second finger from the glove.
- Cut out two butterfly wings from a piece of felt and glue one on each side of the glove finger.
- Glue a small black pompom on the fingertip for a head.
- Glue wiggly eyes to the pompon to complete the butterfly.

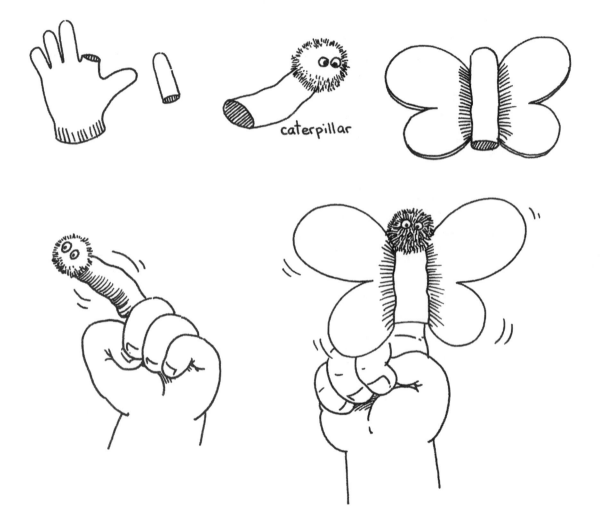

caterpillar

To Use

- Place the caterpillar puppet on a finger of one hand and the butterfly puppet on a finger of the other hand.
- Use the cotton ball as a cocoon while playing with the puppets or telling the story of how a butterfly develops.

Simple Sock Puppets

 Socks/Pantyhose

Materials
socks
non-toxic permanent markers (adults only)

To Make
■ Use permanent markers to draw simple facial features on the toe end of the socks.

To Use
■ Children place the socks on their hands and use their puppets to act out the following rhyme.

Little Puppet

Little puppet, little puppet,
Touch my toes.
Then fly up and land on my nose.

Little puppet, little puppet,
Find my knees.
Now find my elbows
And kiss them, please.

Little puppet, little puppet,
Fly so high.
Now take time to cover my eyes.

And now, my little puppet friend,
Find my chest.
It's time to take a little rest.

Caterpillar Puppet

 Socks/Pantyhose

Materials

The Very Hungry Caterpillar by Eric Carle
green sock
wiggle eyes
fabric glue
felt in a variety of colors, including red
scissors
poster board
markers

To Make

- Glue wiggle eyes onto the toe portion of the green sock.
- Cut out a mouth or tongue from red felt and glue it into place on the sock.
- Use colored felt to make a small butterfly.
- Turn the caterpillar puppet inside out and attach the butterfly to the toe of the sock using fabric glue.
- Use poster board, scissors, and markers to make all of the food the caterpillar in the book eats. Make the foods large enough to cut a hand-size hole into the center of each piece.

turn sock
inside out...

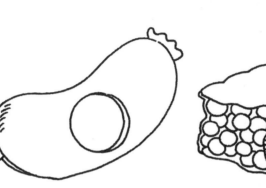

To Use

- Place the puppet on your arm before beginning the story.
- As you read the story, place the items the caterpillar ate over the puppet and onto your arm.
- At the end of the story, turn the caterpillar inside out to reveal the butterfly.

Creative Art

Sponge Print Pictures

Bags

Materials
sponges
scissors
brown paper grocery bags
paint
shallow pans, such as aluminum pie tins

To Make
- Cut sponges into theme-related shapes.
- Cut off the wide sides from brown paper grocery bags.
- Pour paint into shallow pans.

To Use
- Children dip the sponges into the paint and make prints on the brown paper.

Masterpiece in a Bag

Bags

Materials
paper lunch bags
variety of collage materials
cardboard pieces
glue
scissors

To Make
- Fill each lunch bag with a variety of collage materials.
- Cut the cardboard pieces into squares in a variety of sizes up to 12" x 12".

- Place bags, glue, and cardboard squares on the art table.

To Use

- Children choose materials in the bags to glue onto the cardboard squares to make unique collages.

Bag Heads

 Bags

Materials

large paper grocery bags
newspapers
tape
art supplies, such as paint, markers, and crayons

To Make

- Stuff the bag with crumpled newspapers.
- Fold down the opening and tape it securely in place.

To Use

- Children use art supplies to make faces on the bags. The faces might be their own face, friend or family faces, or storybook characters.

Bag Hat

 Bags

Materials

brown paper grocery bag
paint, crayons, and markers
collage materials
glue

To Make

- Fold the opening of the grocery bag until the hat fits a child's head.

To Use

- Children use paint, crayons, markers, glue, and collage materials to decorate the hat.
- They may wear the hats to act out stories or celebrate a special occasion.

Birdseed Bag Pictures

 Bags

Materials

large birdseed bag
scissors
glue
large boxes, optional

To Make

■ Cut out pictures from the outside layer of the bags, since the inside layer may have oily spots from the sunflower and thistle seeds.

To Use

■ Children can glue the pictures on large boxes for child-sized birdhouses, or you can use them in the classroom for a bird-related theme.

Yarn Organizer Bag

 Teacher Tip

 Bags

Materials

mesh produce bag
balls of yarn
pipe cleaner

To Make

■ Place balls of yarn inside a mesh produce bag.
■ Twist a pipe cleaner through the open end of the bag to form a loop for hanging.

To Use

■ Hang the bag using the pipe cleaner loop.
■ Thread yarn strands through the holes in the bag. Pull out yarn to the desired length and cut.

Box Collages

 Boxes

Materials
boxes with lids
tape
collage materials, such as stickers, buttons, paper scraps, felt scraps, textured fabric, and feathers
glue
hole punch
nylon fishing line

To Make
- Tape the lids on the boxes.
- Provide a variety of collage materials and glue.

To Use
- Children glue collage materials to each side of the box.
- Punch a hole into one corner of the box and thread fishing line through the hole.
- Hang the boxes from the ceiling to display.

Box Painting

 Boxes

Materials
cardboard boxes with lids
newspapers
tape
paint
paintbrushes and sponges
glue
paper scraps
paper and marker or pen

To Make
- Stuff boxes with crumpled newspapers and tape the lids on securely.
- Put out paint, brushes, sponges, glue, and paper scraps.

To Use
- Children paint the boxes and glue on paper scraps to decorate.
- Write down the children's dictations or stories about the boxes. Display their written words with the boxes.

Rolling Printers

 Boxes

Materials
cylinder-shaped boxes (oatmeal, salt, potato chip)
rubber bands
paint
shallow pans
paper

To Make
- Wrap rubber bands around the boxes several times, making plenty of textured spaces.
- Pour paint into shallow pans.

To Use
- Children roll the boxes in the paint and then roll them onto paper, making colorful designs as they roll.

Sponge Painting

 Boxes

Materials
sponges
scissors
glue
plastic film canisters
paint
shallow pans
paper

To Make
- Cut sponges into small pieces or shapes.
- Glue one side of each sponge onto the bottom of a film canister.
- Pour paint into shallow pans.

To Use
- Children hold the film canister, dip the sponge end into paint, and make prints on paper.

Lacing Boxes

 Boxes

Materials
shoeboxes without lids
hole punch
strands of yarn
tape

To Make
- Punch holes into the sides of the shoeboxes.
- Wrap a piece of tape around the ends of each strand of yarn.

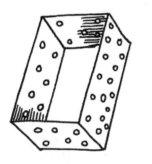 

To Use
- Children lace different colors of yarn through the holes in the sides of the shoebox to make colorful designs.

Hand Prints

 Gloves/Mittens

Materials
mittens and gloves
paint
shallow pans
paper
marker

To Make

- Pour paint into shallow pans.
- Provide a variety of mittens and gloves.

To Use

- Children make mitten prints, glove prints, bare handprints, or any other combination to make colorful designs on paper.
- Note each child's name and the date on individual prints.

Hand Painters

 Gloves/Mittens

Materials

mittens

textured materials, such as a scrubbing sponge, powder puff, lace, nylon bath sponge, terry cloth, or bubble wrap

glue

paint

shallow pans

paper

To Make

- Glue a different texture onto the palm of each mitten.
- Pour paint into shallow pans.

To Use

- Children place a mitten on one hand.
- They carefully dip the textured part of the mitten into paint and make prints on the paper.

Ice Cube Painting

 Gloves/Mittens

Materials
dry tempera paint
freezer paper
mittens or gloves
ice cubes
marker

To Make
- Sprinkle dry tempera paint onto freezer paper.
- Give each child a pair of mittens or gloves.

To Use
- Children wear mittens or gloves to push ice cubes through the dry paint to make wet, colorful designs on paper. Hang the pieces of freezer paper to dry.
- Always label each creation with the child's name and date.

Texture Rollers

 Socks/Pantyhose

Materials
sock with ribbed cuff
paper towel tube
scissors
glue
paint
shallow pans
paper

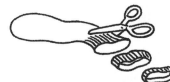 

To Make
- Cut across the sock cuff to make several circles.
- Glue the circles onto the paper towel tube as shown in the illustration.

- Pour a small amount of paint into each pan. Use two or three different colors of paint.

To Use

- Children roll the sock-covered tube into the paint and then roll the tube onto paper to make interesting designs.

Paint Daubers

 Socks/Pantyhose

Materials

pantyhose
scissors
fiberfill
yarn
paint
shallow pans
paper

To Make

- Cut off a 6" length of pantyhose.
- Cut along the length of the 6" pantyhose tube to make a rectangular piece of pantyhose.
- Place a small ball of fiberfill in the center of the rectangle.
- Pull up the edges of the pantyhose and secure them with a piece of yarn.
- Pour paint into shallow pans.

To Use

- Children dip the dauber into the paint and then press the dauber on paper to make colorful designs.

Math and Manipulatives

Graph Book

Bags

Materials

paper and markers (for graphs)
scissors
2-gallon size plastic resealable bags
hole punch
book rings

To Make

- When appropriate, create bar graphs showing classroom events. For example, graph how many children chose different interest areas; how many children are wearing blue, green, white, yellow, or brown shirts; how many children have green, blue, or brown eyes; or what color balls are on the playground.
- Trim the completed graphs to fit inside 2-gallon plastic resealable bags. Put one graph into each bag and seal it closed.
- Punch holes into the left-hand side of the sealed bags.
- Thread the pages onto book rings to make a book.

To Use

- Children "read" the graphs and review the activity as often as they like.

Bear Hunt Game

 Bags

Materials
brown paper grocery bags
scissors
black construction paper
glue
craft knife (adults only)
large cardboard box
markers or paint
tape
giant die

To Make
- Cut out large paw prints from the brown paper bags.
- Cut out paw pads from black construction paper pads and glue them onto the paws.
- Away from the children, use a craft knife to remove one side of the cardboard box.
- Decorate the box using markers or paint to look like a cave.
- Tape the paw prints to the floor to form a path to the box cave, which is at the end of the path.

To Use
- Children roll a die and "bear-walk" the rolled number of steps along the path toward the bear cave.
- After the children have played the game this way for a while, add a blue paper river to swim across, a cardboard box bridge to march across, shredded paper for tall grass to push through, and a climbing piece of equipment for a mountain to climb over to add a challenge as children act out "I'm Going on a Bear Hunt."

Humpty Dumpty Puzzle Bag

Bags

Materials
cardboard
scissors
markers
paper lunch bags
rectangular-shaped sponge
red paint

To Make
- Cut out a large egg shape from a piece of cardboard.
- Use markers to decorate the egg shape to look like Humpty Dumpty.
- Cut the shape into the number of puzzle pieces that is age-appropriate.
- Dip a rectangular-shaped sponge into red paint and make a brick wall pattern on the sides of the paper lunch bag.
- When the paint is dry, place the Humpty Dumpty puzzle pieces inside.

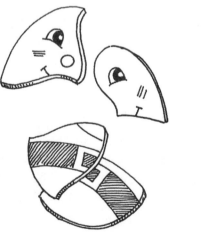

To Use
- Children put the individual puzzle pieces together to make the picture of Humpty Dumpty.

Elephant Bag Counting

 Bags

Materials

gray, black, and white construction paper
marker
scissors
glue
paper lunch bag
blank index cards
peanut-shaped packaging material
clothespins

To Make

- Draw an elephant's head on a piece of gray construction paper. Cut it out.
- Use black and white construction paper to make eyes for the elephant. Glue them onto the elephant's face.
- Fold the opening of the bag down, leaving a large opening.
- Glue the elephant's face onto one wide side of the bag.
- Write a numeral and the same number of dots on each index card.

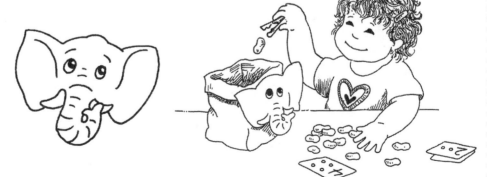

To Use

- Shuffle the cards and turn them face down.
- Children choose a card and use a clothespin to "feed" the appropriate number of "peanuts" into the bag.

Bunny Bag Counting

Bags

Materials

white construction paper
scissors
markers
paper lunch bags
glue
orange and green construction paper

To Make

- Cut out as many white construction paper bunnies as is age or stage appropriate for the children.
- Write the appropriate numerals on each bunny and glue each bunny onto a separate bag.
- Cut out the same number of orange construction paper carrots as bunnies.
- Cut out leaves from green construction paper and glue them to the carrot shapes.
- Make large dots on the carrots to match the numerals on the bunny bags.

To Use

- Children count the dots on the carrots, match the carrot with the appropriate bunny bag, and drop the carrot inside the bunny bag.

Hint: Use other animals with appropriate foods for additional theme-related units.

Spider Counting

 Bags

Materials

paper lunch bags
old newspapers
yarn
black paint
paintbrush
black crepe paper streamers
white paper
scissors
glue

To Make

- Stuff the paper bag with old newspapers and tie the opening closed with a short length of yarn.
- Paint the bag using black paint. When the paint is dry, tape eight black crepe paper legs onto the body.
- Cut out two circles from white paper to make eyes. Glue them to the bag and use black paint to complete the eyes.
- Attach a long length of yarn to the top of the spider and hang the spiders, so their legs are hanging down within reach of children.

To Use

- Children practice their counting skills using the spider's legs.

Which Box Is Missing?

 Boxes

Materials
4-6 different sizes and shapes of boxes
contact paper
scarf

To Make
- Cover the boxes with different colors of contact paper.
- Place the boxes on a table.

To Use
- Cover the boxes with a scarf and remove a box without the children seeing which one is taken away.
- Remove the cloth and see if the children can guess which box is missing.

Cereal Box Graphing

 Boxes

Materials
butcher paper
markers
empty cereal boxes

To Make
- Draw a graph on a piece of butcher paper.
- Place the butcher paper on the floor.
- Place the cereal boxes on the floor.

To Use

- Children sort the cereal boxes by name, size of boxes, colors, and so on, and then place them in rows on the butcher paper.
- Help the children count the boxes and make comparisons of more and less.
- Use markers to write numerals on the butcher paper graph.

Sorting Sizes Boxes

 Boxes

Materials

small, medium, and large detergent and toothpaste boxes
colored contact paper
sticky labels
permanent marker (adults only)

To Make

- Cover the boxes with colored contact paper.
- Label each box "small," "medium," or "large" using sticky labels and a permanent marker.
- Place all of the boxes inside the large detergent box.

To Use

- Children line up the boxes according to size.
- Help them use the vocabulary words *small, medium, and large* as they play.

Rock Sorter

 Boxes

Materials

shoebox with lid
craft knife (adults only)
different sizes of rocks

To Make

- Away from the children, use a craft knife to cut several different sizes of holes into the box lid.
- Place the lid on the box.

To Use

- Put the box and a number of different sizes of rocks on a table. Children sort the rocks and put them into the appropriate size holes. Then they open the box, remove the rocks, and begin again.

Caution: Supervise closely.

Band-Aid Box Sorting

 Boxes

Materials

glue
box of assorted sizes of Band-Aids
index cards
box or basket

To Make

- Glue one of each size of Band-Aids to an index card.
- Open the remaining Band-Aids, leaving the backing strips on.
- Place the index cards and opened Band-Aids inside a box or basket.

To Use

- Children match Band-Aids of the same size to the index cards.

Room Sort

 Boxes

Materials

old magazines
scissors
glue
construction paper
clear contact paper or laminating machine
shoeboxes
art supplies

To Make

- Cut out pictures from magazines of items that belong in rooms in a house, such as a bed, kitchen table, chair, and so on.
- Glue the pictures to construction paper squares.
- Laminate the pictures or cover them with clear contact paper.
- Also cut out larger pictures of the different rooms in a house, such as a kitchen, bedroom, and so on.
- Glue the magazine pictures that represent the different rooms in a house to the outside of each shoebox.

To Use

- Children sort the pictures and put them into the appropriate "rooms."

Box of Chocolates Matching

 Boxes

Materials
stickers
heart-shaped candy box with divider in place
plastic bottle caps

To Make
■ Put a different sticker into each compartment in the candy box.
■ Place matching stickers onto the plastic bottle caps.

To Use
■ Children match the bottle caps with the stickers in the compartments of the candy box.

Sorting Train

 Boxes

Materials
shoebox with lid
tape
glue
paper cup
toilet paper tube
spray paint in basic colors (adults only)
diaper wipes boxes
juice can lids

To Make

- To make the train engine, tape the lid onto the shoebox.
- Glue a paper cup upside down near one end of the box.
- Tape a toilet paper tube to the top of the cup for the smokestack.
- Away from the children and in a well-ventilated area, spray paint the engine black and each of the diaper wipe boxes a different basic color.
- While the boxes dry, paint the juice can lids to match the wipes box colors.
- When the cars and lids are dry, line up the train with the engine first and the wipe boxes behind it.

To Use

- Children match the colored lids to the appropriate colored train car.
- Store the lids inside the train cars.

Ping-Pong Ball Scoop

 Boxes

Materials

Ping-Pong balls
permanent marker (adults only)
clean, empty ice cream bucket
ice cream scoop
plastic bowls

To Make

- Write letters, numerals, shapes, or words on the Ping-Pong balls.
- Put the balls inside the ice cream bucket.

To Use

- Children take turns using the ice cream scoop to "dip" a Ping-Pong ball from the bucket.
- One child identifies whatever is on the ball and places it in his bowl.
- If the child is unable to identify what is on the ball, the ball goes back into the bucket.
- When the bucket is empty, children count the balls in their bowls to see how many each child was able to identify.

Ice Cream Cones Matching

 Boxes

Materials

brown felt
scissors
pastel-colored felt
permanent marker (adults only)
commercial ice cream bucket

To Make

- Cut ice cream cone shapes from brown felt.
- Cut the same number of ice cream scoop shapes from pastel colors of felt.
- Use a permanent marker to write matching letters, numerals, or shapes on pairs of cones and scoops of ice cream.
- Place the cones and scoops inside the ice cream bucket.

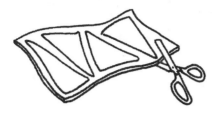

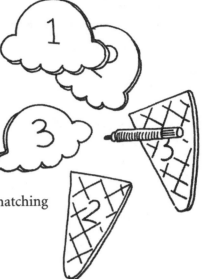

To Use
- Children choose a cone and find the matching ice cream scoop.

Top the Box

 Boxes

Materials
marker
small cardboard jewelry boxes with lids
stickers

To Make
- Remove the lids from the boxes.
- Write a number from one to five on the inside bottom of each box.
- Write the numbers on the inside of the box top, too.
- Place the appropriate number of stickers on top of each lid.

To Use
- Children count the stickers on the box lids and match the lids to the appropriate boxes.

Counting Buckets

 Boxes

Materials

10 clean, fast food buckets
spray paint (adults only)
permanent marker (adults only)
clothespins
55 items for counting

To Make

- Away from the children and in a well-ventilated area, spray paint the buckets.
- When the paint is dry, use a permanent marker to write the numerals 1-10 on the buckets.
- Use clothespins to connect the buckets in a straight line in numeral order.
- Provide 55 items so the children can count out the appropriate number of items for each bucket.

To Use

- Children count the items and place them into the appropriate buckets to practice counting skills. For example, they count out two items to put into the bucket with the number "2."

Dog House Game

 Boxes

Materials
half-pint milk cartons
craft knife (adults only)
paint
paintbrushes
markers
scissors
construction paper
die

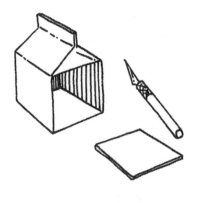

To Make
- Collect an appropriate number of milk cartons that reflect the children's counting ability.
- Away from the children, use a craft knife to cut off one side of the milk cartons.
- Paint the milk cartons to look like doghouses.
- Write numerals or draw the appropriate number of dots onto each doghouse.
- Cut out construction paper dog shapes. Decorate them using markers, if desired.

To Use
- Children roll the die and place the appropriate number of paper dogs inside the appropriate doghouse.

Hungry Pup

 Boxes

Materials

brown paper grocery bag
scissors
tape
shoebox with lid
brown, white, and black construction paper
glue
markers
craft knife (adults only)
colored construction paper

tape the lid on the shoebox... cover with brown paper...

To Make

- Cut off the bottom of the grocery bag and cut the length of one side to make a large piece of flat paper.
- Tape the lid onto the shoebox. Wrap the shoebox with the flat brown paper grocery bag and secure with tape.
- Cut out ears from brown construction paper, eyes from white paper, and whiskers and a nose from black paper.
- Glue the facial features onto the box. Use markers to add more details.
- Away from the children, use a craft knife to cut out a large hole where the dog's mouth should be.
- Cut out a variety of colored construction paper bones.

cut a large hole for dog's mouth...

To Use

- Children "feed" the dog by placing the bones into the dog's mouth and taking them out again.
- Older children may use this as a counting game. Add number cards that tell how many bones to feed the dog.

Owls in the Tree Game

 Boxes

Materials

oatmeal container
construction paper
tape or glue
craft knife (adults only)
index cards
permanent marker (adults only)
toilet paper rolls
scissors

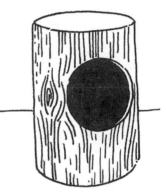

To Make

- Cover an oatmeal container with brown construction paper and tape or glue it in place.
- Away from the children, use a craft knife to cut out a large round hole in the side of the container.
- Number a set of index cards with the numerals 1-10.
- Cut toilet paper rolls into ten rings.
- Use a black marker to add eyes to each ring. Cut out beaks from yellow construction paper and attach them underneath the eyes.

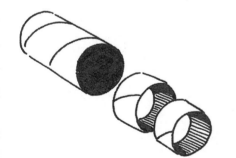  

To Use

- To play the game, the children turn the number cards upside down.
- The children choose a card, identify the number, and place the corresponding number of "owls" into the hole in the oatmeal container "tree."
- Continue to play until all the cards are used.

Go Fish Game

 Boxes

Materials

cardboard box
construction paper
glue
craft knife (adults only)
poster board
scissors
paper clips
string
magnet
paper towel or wrapping paper tube

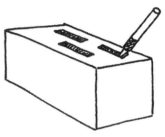

To Make

- Turn a cardboard box upside down and completely cover it with blue paper. Glue it in place.
- Away from the children, use a craft knife to cut several slits into the sides and bottom of the box.
- Cut out fish shapes from poster board.
- Place a paper clip on each fish.
- Tie a magnet onto one end of a piece of string and tie the other end to a paper towel or wrapping paper tube to make a fishing pole and line.
- Place the poster board fish into the slits in the box.

To Use

- The children "fish" by dropping the magnet into a slot in the box. The magnet will attach to a paper clip on the fish.

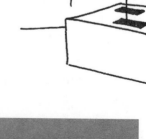

Exploring Mittens and Gloves

 Gloves/Mittens

Materials
mittens and gloves
box or basket
chart paper
markers

To Make
- Place a variety of sizes, styles, and textures of mittens and gloves in a box or basket.

To Use
- Children try on the gloves and mittens.
- Talk with the children about the textures and sizes of the gloves and mittens, and about which ones are easy to put on and which ones are hard to put on.
- Interact with children as they explore the mittens and gloves.
- Make a chart dividing the gloves and mittens into categories of the children's choosing.

Comparing Mittens

 Gloves/Mittens

Materials
chart paper
markers
variety of sizes of mittens made with different materials
basket

To Make

- Draw a graph that has pictures of mittens on a piece of chart paper.
- Place mittens in a basket near the graph.

To Use

- Each child experiments with the mittens and chooses the mittens he thinks are warmest.
- Mark the graph to show each child's choice.
- Talk about the graph, comparing which mittens were chosen to be the warmest and which were not chosen.

Sorting Socks and Mittens

 Gloves/Mittens

Socks/Pantyhose

Materials

different colors, sizes, and patterns of socks and mittens
basket

To Make

- Place socks and mittens of different sizes and types into a basket.

To Use

- Children place the socks or mittens in order from smallest to largest.
- Children sort the socks or mittens by size, color, and pattern.

Sorting Laundry

 Socks/Pantyhose

Materials
pairs of socks (matching colors or matching sizes)
laundry basket
clothesline
clothespins

To Make
- Place unmatched pairs of socks into a laundry basket.
- Hang a clothesline in the classroom.

To Use
- Children match socks by color or size.
- Add interest by providing clothespins so the children can hang up the socks.

Weighing Socks

 Socks/Pantyhose

Materials
socks
various materials, such as dry rice, dry beans, marbles, cotton balls, or shredded paper
balance scale

To Make
- Fill the socks with different materials such as dry rice, beans, marbles, cotton balls, or shredded paper.
- Tie a knot in the opening of each sock.

To Use
- Children pick up and feel the weight of each sock.
- They determine which socks weigh the same, which socks are heavier, and which socks are lighter.
- Show the children how to use the balance scale to determine which of two socks is heavier or lighter.

Dramatic Play

Stuffed Bag Apples, Pumpkins, and Turkeys

 Bags

Materials
paper lunch bags and large grocery bags
old newspapers
yarn
brown, green, orange, and red paint
paintbrush
black marker
scissors
construction paper
glue

To Make
- Stuff the bags with crumpled old newspapers.
- Tie the openings closed with yarn.
- To make an apple, paint the top brown or green for a stem and paint the stuffed part of the bag red or green for the apple.
- To make a pumpkin, paint the stuffed part of the bag orange and paint the twisted top green to make a stem. To create a jack-o-lantern, wait for the paint to dry. Then use a black marker to make facial features on the bag.
- To create a turkey, cut out a turkey head from red construction paper and cut out tail feathers from different colors of construction paper. Glue the feathers onto the open end of the bag and glue the head on the opposite end of the bag.

To Use
- Use the stuffed apples, pumpkins, and turkeys as a part of the theme-related decorations in dramatic play or as an extension of discussions in group time.

Big Bag Feet

 Bags

Materials
4 large paper grocery bags
old newspapers
glue
craft knife (adult only)
construction paper
scissors

To Make
- Lightly stuff a grocery bag with old newspapers.
- Slide a second bag over the open end of the stuffed bag and glue it in place.
- Away from the children, use a craft knife to cut out an oval-shaped hole near the end of the bag big enough for a child's foot to fit through.
- Cut out toes from construction paper and glue them to the end of the bag opposite the hole.
- Repeat the process to make a second foot.

To Use
- Outside on the grass, children slip their feet into the holes in the bags and walk while holding the teacher's or another child's hand. Decorate shoes and add face paint and a funny hat to create a clown costume.

Paper Bag Costumes

 Bags

Materials
large paper grocery bags
paint
paintbrushes
scissors

art materials
construction paper
fancy-edge scissors
tape

To Make

- Paint the bags to look like an animal or storybook character (without a face).
- Cut out half ovals from each narrow side of a bag, so the bag will sit on a child's shoulders.
- Cut out a face-size opening in the front of the bag so the children can see.
- Decorate the bags using art materials.
- To make curly hair, use fancy-edge scissors to cut long, narrow strips of construction paper. Pull the strips across the flat side of the blade of regular scissors to make them curl. Tape them to the top of the bag.

To Use

- Children wear the costumes to role-play characters.

Animal Costumes

 Bags

Materials

large brown paper bags
scissors
construction paper
cardboard tubes or paper cups
glue
paint and brushes
art supplies
pantyhose
tape
paper lunch bags
string

To Make

- To make animal masks, cut out a large circle for a child's face on one wide side of a bag. Then cut out half ovals from each narrow side of a bag, so the bag will sit on a child's shoulders.
- Cut out noses, ears, or horns from construction paper, or use paper cups or cardboard tubes. Glue them onto the bag.
- Use paint and other art supplies to complete the masks.
- Cut construction paper into strips and glue them on top of the mask for hair or lion manes.
- Braid pantyhose for tails and attach them with tape to the backside of the mask.
- To make paws, slip small paper lunch bags over the child's hands and feet and tie them with string.

To Use

- Children place the mask over their heads and role-play the animal.

Stick Donkey

Bags

Materials

construction paper
scissors
glue
large paper grocery bag
newspaper
long gift-wrap tube
string or tape
yarn

To Make

- Cut out ears from construction paper and glue them onto the wide sides of the grocery bag, near the top of the bag. Make sure to crease the ears before gluing them on.
- Draw a donkey face on the bag (see illustration).
- Stuff the grocery bag with newspaper and fasten it onto the cardboard tube with string or tape.
- Glue yarn on the donkey head to make mane.
- Cut out several lengths of yarn. Tie one end of the strands together and fasten them onto the end of the cardboard tube for a tail.

To Use

- Children ride the donkey to role-play.

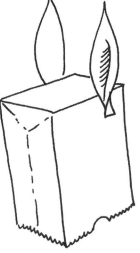

crease the ear before gluing...

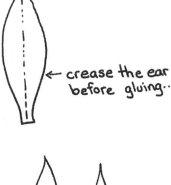

Prop Boxes

The following are examples of dramatic play prop boxes. Make a list of the contents of each box and attach it to the underside of the lid. Label the box on the end that will be visible when the box is in storage (usually on a shelf). Use your imagination to think of other prop boxes that children will enjoy.

 Boxes

Materials
copy paper box (one for each prop box)
paint
paintbrushes

Florist Prop Box
silk flowers
plastic vases
gift cards
baskets
colorful tissue paper
ribbons/bows
paint

Bank Prop Box
play money
cash register
deposit slips
pens/pencils
bank sign
purses/wallets
lock box
rings of keys

Bakery Prop Box
playdough (teacher-made and commercial)
rolling pins
small pans
muffin tins
cookie cutters
birthday decorations

chef hats
aprons
oven mitts
paint

Beach Prop Box
paint
beach umbrella
beach towels
sunglasses
empty suntan lotion bottles
sand buckets/shovels
beach balls
sun hats
toy radios
child-size beach chairs

To Make

- Paint the outside of the box to represent its contents (florist, bank, bakery, beach).
- Place gathered items into each box.

To Use

- Children use the box of materials to role-play experiences in a flower shop, a bank, a bakery, or at the beach.

Fireplace

 Boxes

Materials

large cardboard appliance box
tape
craft knife (adults only)
rectangular sponge
red tempera paint
newspapers

To Make

- Close all the openings of the large box and secure them with tape.
- Away from the children, use a craft knife to cut out a fireplace opening in one side of the box.
- Dip a rectangular sponge into red paint and make brick prints on the box.
- Roll newspapers into log shapes and secure the edges with tape.

To Use

- Use the fireplace as part of the decorations for dramatic play.
- Children build a pretend fire in the fireplace with the newspaper "logs" or decorate the fireplace for the holidays.

Cash Register

 Boxes

Materials

sponges
scissors
permanent marker (adults only)
glue
shoebox with lid
play money

To Make

- Cut sponges into small squares.
- Use a permanent marker to write numerals on each sponge.
- Glue the sponges onto the shoebox lid to look like a cash register keypad.
- Store play money inside the box.

To Use

- Children use the pretend cash register to role-play being a cashier. In addition to using this as a prop in dramatic play, use it in the math area for some practical math experiences.

Elephant Friend

 Boxes

Materials

large cardboard box
craft knife (adults only)
tape
stapler
fabric strips
paint
paintbrushes
yarn

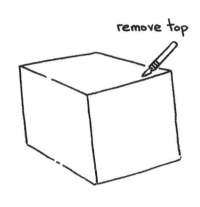

remove top

To Make

- Away from the children, use a craft knife to remove the top of the box.
- Turn the box upside down and tape the bottom securely closed.
- Away from the children, use a craft knife to cut out a large square in the bottom of the box.
- Staple two strips of fabric across the square opening to make shoulder straps.
- Paint the box to look like an elephant.
- Use the leftover cardboard from the top to make an elephant's head.
- Paint the head to match the body and add facial features.
- Staple the head to one side of the box.
- Braid several strands of yarn to make a tail. Tape the tail in place.

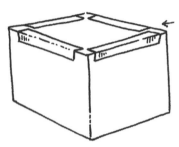

- turn box over and tape bottom securely....

cut out a large square..

To Use

- A child puts his head through the square opening, allowing the fabric straps to rest on his shoulders.
- The costume allows a child to role-play being an elephant (or any other animal you might create). Take the box animals outside so the children have plenty of room to play.

Big Boat

 Boxes

Materials

large rectangular cardboard boxes
duct tape
craft knife (adults only)
cardboard
scissors
wrapping paper rolls
glue
paint
paintbrushes
blue butcher paper

To Make

- Remove any staples from the box and cover any rough edges with wide duct tape.
- Away from the children, use a craft knife to remove one wide side of the box.
- Secure any flaps with tape.
- Place the box on the floor with the open side up.
- Cut out paddles from cardboard (see illustration on the next page).
- Away from the children, use a craft knife to cut slots into one end of each wrapping paper tube (see illustration on the next page). Slide the cardboard paddles into the slots and glue them in place.
- Encourage the children to join in the fun of painting the boats and paddles.

To Use

- Spread a large sheet of blue butcher paper on the floor to represent water. Children sit in the boat and role-play a boat ride.
- Place the boat in the dramatic play area or take it outside for a new outdoor experience.

Big Bus

 Boxes

Materials

large refrigerator box
craft knife (adults only)
large cube-shaped box
7 cardboard pizza boards (from frozen pizza boxes)
yellow and black paint
paintbrushes
bolts and nuts
old newspapers

To Make

- Turn the refrigerator box on its side to make the main body of the bus.
- Away from the children, use a craft knife to cut out rectangular windows in the wide sides of the box.

- Place a large cube-shaped box at one end of the refrigerator carton for the front of the bus.
- Away from the children, use the craft knife to cut out front windows.
- Paint the pizza boards with black paint.
- Attach one pizza board in the cab of the bus using a bolt and nut for the steering wheel.
- Attach a set of wheels on the cab and two sets on the main part of the bus.
- Place old newspapers underneath the bus or bring it outside and paint the bus yellow.

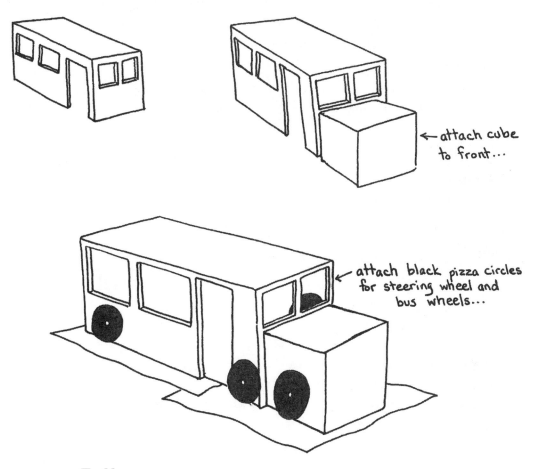

←attach cube to front...

←attach black pizza circles for steering wheel and bus wheels...

To Use

- Children pretend to drive or ride the bus. Place small chairs or pillows inside the bus for seats.
- Teach the children "Wheels on the Bus" as they play.

Elegant Evening Wear

 Gloves/Mittens

Materials

elegant evening wear, such as long evening gloves, old dance recital costumes, fancy purses, small-size short evening dresses, dress shoes, plastic tiaras and necklaces, feather boas, small men's suits, assorted jackets, and cloth flowers for corsages or boutonnieres

To Make

- Gather a variety of fancy, elegant evening wear, complete with long gloves.

To Use

- Children dress up in the fancy clothing and act out imaginative roles.

Note from the Authors

Thrift stores are a great source for inexpensive dress-up clothing of all types. Additionally, parents can be a wonderful source for dress-up clothing. Use small adult sizes or large children/teen sizes, so clothing will be easy to get on and off over a child's clothing. Avoid clothing that a child will trip over or have difficulty keeping on. Always provide a place to hang clothing. (Pegs work best.) For clothing that is too long, simply cut to the correct lengths or use duct tape for a quick hem.

Fancy Gloves

 Gloves/Mittens

Materials

women's and men's gloves
buttons
needle and thread (adults only)
fabric paint
satin ribbons
dress-up clothing

To Make

- Securely sew colorful buttons onto pairs of women's gloves.
- Decorate the pairs of gloves using shiny fabric paint and colored satin ribbons.

To Use

- Children use the fancy gloves with dress-up clothing as they act out different roles.

Sock Dolls

 Socks/Pantyhose

Materials

tube socks
fiberfill
fabric paint
paintbrush
small baby blankets

To Make

- Stuff a tube sock with fiberfill.
- Tie a knot in the opening of the sock.
- Use fabric paint to make a face and create hair for the doll.

To Use

- Children wrap the soft, cuddly dolls in blankets as they role-play taking care of babies.

Pantyhose Wig

 Socks/Pantyhose

Materials

3 pairs of pantyhose
scissors
yarn

To Make

- Cut off the legs of two pairs of clean, old pantyhose.
- Tie two pantyhose legs to each leg of a third pair of clean, old pantyhose. Braid each leg and tie the ends with yarn to make pigtails.

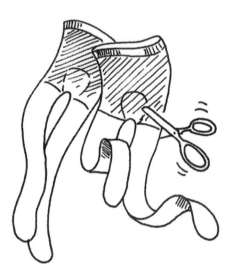

To Use

- Children place the panty portion of the pantyhose on their head for a wig with pigtails.

Pantyhose Masks

 Socks/pantyhose

Materials

pantyhose
scissors
wire coat hangers
duct tape
paint
paintbrushes
art materials

To Make

- Cut off one leg from a pair of pantyhose.
- Bend the wire coat hangers into a desired shape, twisting the hook portion into a handle.
- Stretch the pantyhose leg over the wire frame and secure with duct tape.
- Cover any sharp edges of the coat hanger with layers of duct tape.
- Cut out eyes, nose, and mouth openings in the mask.
- Use paint and other art materials to decorate the mask.

To Use

- Children hold the masks in front of their faces to act out stories.

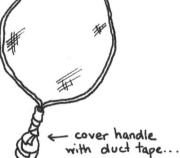

← cover handle with duct tape...

Blocks and Construction

Paper Bag People

Bags

Materials

2 brown paper grocery bags
old newspapers
tape
art supplies
glue

To Make

- Stuff one bag with crumpled newspaper.
- Slip the other bag over the stuffed bag and tape it into place.
- Use art supplies and glue to decorate the bags to look like people.

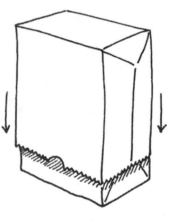

To Use
- Bag people are fun to use in the blocks and construction areas to inspire and enhance children's creations.

Lunch Bag City

 Bags

Materials
paper lunch bags
markers
newspapers
tape

To Make
- Use markers to draw houses, businesses, municipal buildings, and other buildings on paper lunch bags.
- Stuff the bags with crumpled newspapers.
- Tape the openings securely closed.

To Use
- Children use the bags to create a city with block roads, people figures, signs, and vehicles.
- Talk with the children about what they are building.
- Offer to write their stories on chart paper as they play out their stories in the construction area.

Advertising Signs

 Bags

Materials

poster board
scissors
fast-food restaurant bags
glue
tape
paint mixing sticks
clay

To Make

- Cut poster board into squares.
- Cut out logos from the fast-food bags and glue them onto the poster board squares.
- Tape the signs to paint mixing sticks.
- Anchor the signs in a large ball of clay.

To Use

- Place signs in the block area as enrichments for children's creative building.

Box Houses

Boxes

Materials

food boxes in a variety of sizes
newspaper
tape
glue
paint
paintbrushes

To Make

- Stuff food boxes with crumpled newspaper and tape the openings securely closed.
- Glue boxes together to make a desired house shape.
- Paint the houses.

To Use

- Children use the completed houses to make a town.

Quiet Corners

 Boxes

Materials

square cardboard box, large enough for one or two children to sit in
craft knife (adults only)
markers
paint
paintbrushes
square pillow

To Make

- Away from the children, use a craft knife to cut off the top and one side of a large box.
- Children can paint the box and use markers to decorate it.
- Place a square pillow inside.

To Use

- Children sit in the box for quiet activities or for privacy. This creates a great place for children to be alone and get away from the noise and activity of the classroom.

Science

Nesting Ball

Bags

Materials

nesting materials, such as dryer lint, small pieces of yarn or fabric,
   and paper scraps
mesh produce bag
string

To Make

- Stuff the nesting material into the mesh bag.
- Tie the bag closed with string.

To Use

- Hang the Nesting Ball from a tree branch with a loop of string
  or yarn.
- Children watch for birds taking the materials from the ball to
  make a nest.
- After a few days, walk around the area to see if the children can
  see any of the materials woven into a nest.

Growing Corn

Bags

Materials

resealable plastic bag
potting soil
dried corn kernels (seeds)
water

To Make

- Pour potting soil into the bag.
- Place two or three corn kernels (seeds) in the soil. (Cooked corn
  kernels will not sprout. Also, avoid commercial popcorn since
  added ingredients may also keep kernels from sprouting.)

- Sprinkle the soil with water.
- Seal the bag and hang it in a sunny window.

To Use
- Children watch as the seeds sprout (in about a week).

Window Greenhouse

 Bags

Materials
paper towels
water
resealable plastic bags
seeds
yarn
clothespins
sponge
clear salad container

To Make
- Place a wet paper towel inside each plastic bag.
- Sprinkle fast-growing seeds onto the paper towels.
- Seal the bags closed.
- Stretch a length of yarn across a sunny window.
- Use clothespins to hang the sealed bags from the length of yarn.
- Make another type of greenhouse by sprinkling seeds onto a damp sponge. Then place the sponge into a clear salad container and place it in a sunny window.

To Use
- Children observe the seeds sprouting and growing.
- Make the activity more interesting by allowing the children to choose seeds and plant them on their own. Label each bag with the child's name and the date.

Sea Bags

Bags

Materials

sand

shells

colorful rocks

sea animal shapes

plastic tub

small resealable plastic bags

paper and pen

To Make

- Place sand, shells, colorful rocks, and sea animal shapes into a plastic tub. Encourage the children to explore the items in the science area.
- Pour a small amount of sand inside each bag and give one to each child.
- The children can choose shells, rocks, and animal shapes to add to their bags.
- Glue and tape the bags securely closed.

To Use

- Children experience the real seashore materials as they make their own tiny piece of the beach. Ask each child to dictate to you a story about what is in the bag. Share the bags and stories with parents.

Sink or Float Bags

Bags

Materials
resealable plastic bags
variety of items that sink and items that float
water
duct tape
plastic tub
2 boxes
markers

To Make
- Place items that sink and items that float into individual plastic resealable bags.
- Fill each bag half full with water.
- Seal the bags and securely tape the openings to prevent spills.
- Place the bags in a plastic tub.
- Label one box "sink" and one box "float."

To Use
- Children look at the bags and decide if the item in the bag is floating or sinking.
- They place the bags in the appropriately labeled box.

Squish Bags

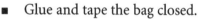 Bags

Materials

heavy-duty resealable plastic bags

white or clear smooth-textured products, such as non-
  toxic hair gel or shaving cream, whipping cream, and
  dessert topping

food coloring

duct tape

glue

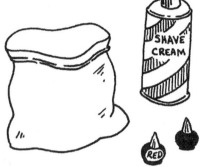

To Make

- Place some of the white or clear product into a plastic bag.
- Squirt a few drops of food coloring onto the product in the bag.
- Add more of the white or clear product, so the food coloring is surrounded.
- Glue and tape the bag closed.

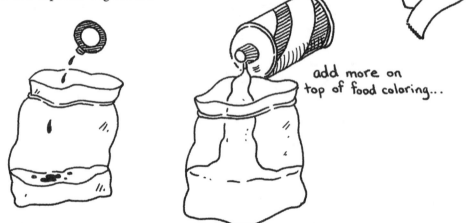

add more on top of food coloring...

To Use

- Children squeeze the bag to observe the color changes in the bag.
- As a variation, squirt two different colors of food coloring into the bag, so the children can squeeze the bags to make new colors.

Sensory Bag

Bags

Materials
2 resealable plastic freezer bags
hair styling or setting gel
glue
duct tape
refrigerator

To Make
- Fill two resealable plastic bags with hair gel.
- Seal the bags closed with glue and a strip of duct tape.
- Place one bag into the refrigerator until well chilled.
- Place the other bag in a sunny window until it is pleasantly warm.

To Use
- Children squeeze, squish, and pat the bags to experience the differences in temperature.

Mixing Bags

Bags

Materials
1 cup cornstarch (125 g)
⅓ cup sugar (40 g)
4 cups water (1 liter)
mixing spoon
pan
stove or hot plate (adults only)
resealable freezer bags
food coloring
tape

To Make

- Mix the cornstarch, sugar, and water in a pan. Cook over medium heat until thick. (This step should be done by an adult, away from the children.)
- Remove the mixture from the heat and allow it to cool. When it is cool, separate into thirds.
- Place each third into a separate plastic freezer bag.
- Add 1 tablespoon of food coloring to the mixture in each plastic freezer bag.
- Seal and tape each bag closed.

To Use

- Children squeeze the bags and observe how the colors change and mix.

Stuffed Bag Whale

Bags

Materials
paper lunch bags
old newspapers
tape
blue or gray paint
paintbrush
construction paper
scissors
glue
aluminum foil

To Make

- Stuff a lunch bag with crumpled newspaper, twist the opening closed, and tape it securely shut.
- Paint the bag with blue or gray paint.
- When the paint is dry, cut out eyes from construction paper and glue them onto the bag.
- Cut aluminum foil into short, narrow strips and shape them to look like a waterspout.
- Tape the foil waterspout in place on the whale.

To Use
- Children use the whales in their explorations of whales, large animals, and/or mammals. Place them in the science, blocks, or even dramatic play area.

Recycling Center

 Boxes

Materials
large cardboard boxes
markers

To Make
- Use markers to label each box for the type of recyclable materials to be placed inside it. Many cities provide opportunities to recycle aluminum, glass, plastic, and paper.
- Research recycling in your area to determine what the requirements are for recycling different materials.

To Use
- Children bring recyclable materials from home and sort them into the appropriate boxes. If materials are to be sold, plan how the proceeds will be spent (for example, class materials, charities, or a special field trip).

Hanging Garden

 Boxes

Materials
clean, half-pint milk or juice carton
craft knife (adults only)
hole punch
string
potting soil
seeds
water

To Make

- Away from the children, use a craft knife to cut off the top of the carton.
- Use a hole punch to punch a hole into each side of the carton.
- Tie a length of string through the holes and tie the ends together to create a hanger.
- Fill the carton with potting soil and quick-growing seeds.
- Moisten with water and hang in a sunny window.

To Use

- Children watch the plants grow.
- Children may sketch the progress of the plants or dictate their observations.

Bird Feeder

 Boxes

Materials

empty, clean small milk carton
tape
craft knife (adults only)
hole punch
yarn
birdseed

To Make

- Tape the milk carton closed.
- Away from the children, use a craft knife to cut out one side of the carton, leaving an inch or so at the bottom.
- Punch a hole into the top of the box and tie a yarn loop through the hole.

To Use

- Children fill the bottom of the feeder with birdseed and hang it from a tree or shrub.
- Children may keep a picture journal of birds that visit the feeder.

Windmill

 Boxes

Materials

clean, half-gallon milk carton
craft knife (adults only)
hole punch
string

To Make

- Away from the children, use a craft knife to cut a vertical door into each side of a half-gallon carton.
- Cut the doors so they will all open in the same direction.
- Fold the doors so they will stay open.
- Punch a hole into the top of the carton and tie a piece of string through the hole.

cut door on all four sides

To Use

- Hang the windmill outside and watch it twirl.

Texture Glove

Gloves/Mittens

Materials

textured fabric scraps, such as velvet, corduroy, and silk
scissors
cotton glove
needle and thread (adults only)
textured buttons

To Make

- Cut the textured fabrics into fingertip-size pieces.
- Sew a different textured fabric onto each fingertip of the glove.
- Attach textured buttons to some of the fingertips.

To Use

- A child places the glove on her hand and then explores the textures.
- Talk about soft, rough, bumpy, or scratchy as children touch each texture.
- Interact with the children as they explore the textures.

Sock Garden

 Socks/Pantyhose

Materials

discarded large tube socks
aluminum baking pans
potting soil
water

To Make

- Each child pulls a tube sock over her shoe and stretches it up her leg.
- Take the children outside for a walk in a grassy field with weeds.

To Use

- After the walk, the children carefully remove their socks and place them into shallow pans of potting soil.
- Lightly cover the socks with additional soil and dampen them with water.
- Place the pans in a sunny place.
- Children water their "garden," watch for sprouts, and observe the kinds of plants that grow.
- As a variation, after the children take off their socks, spray them with water and place them into resealable plastic bags. Seal the bags closed. Label each one with the child's name and the date. Hang them in a sunny window.

Bug Keeper

 Socks/Pantyhose

Materials

2-liter plastic bottle or half-gallon milk carton
craft knife (adults only)
pantyhose
scissors
grass clippings, twigs, and leaves
water
cotton ball
yarn

To Make

- Away from the children, use a craft knife to cut off the neck of a 2-liter plastic bottle and cut large openings in the sides of the bottle. Or cut off the top of a half-gallon milk container and cut large rectangles in the sides of the jug.
- Cut off one leg from a pair of pantyhose.

To Use

- Children place grass clippings, twigs, leaves, and a wet cotton ball inside the bottle and then place it inside a length of pantyhose.
- Take the children outside to capture a "bug." (Caution the children to allow you to check insects for safety before they touch them.) The children put the insect inside the bottle and fasten the top of the pantyhose with a piece of yarn.
- After a day or so of observing the creature, the children can open the top and allow it to go free.
- This can lead into excellent language arts activities. Children can dictate their observations to you. Write the children's comments about "creatures" on chart paper during group time. Children can draw the creatures and tell stories about them.

Feel-y Can

 Socks/Pantyhose

Materials

coffee can with a plastic lid

craft knife (adults only)

scissors

sock

stapler

duct tape

materials with a variety of textures, such as velvet or velour cloth, sandpaper, and a smooth ball

To Make

- Away from the children, use a craft knife to cut out a circle from the plastic lid.
- Cut off the cuff part of a sock.
- Put the cuff through the hole in the lid.
- Use a stapler to attach the sock to the lid and cover the staples with duct tape.
- Place textured materials inside the can and put the lid in place.

To Use

- Children put their hand inside the sock cuff and touch the textured materials.
- Talk with the children about how each object feels.
- Encourage the children to guess what the object is that they are feeling.

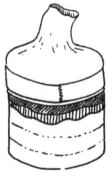

Sand and Water

Water Scopes

 Boxes

Materials
colorful plastic fish
clear, plastic deli containers

To Make
- Place colorful fish in the bottom of the water table.

To Use
- Children place the plastic containers on top of the water and look through them to see the fish underneath the water.

Salt Box Pouring

 Boxes

Materials
salt box
craft knife (adults only)

To Make
- Away from the children, use a craft knife to cut off the bottom of the salt box.

To Use
- Children turn the box upside down and hold the spout closed.
- They fill the box with sand.
- Then they open the spout and allow the sand to flow through the spout.

Powder Box Sprinkler

 Boxes

Materials
empty, clean, plastic powder container
craft knife (adults only)
duct tape

To Make
- Away from the children, use a craft knife to cut off the bottom of the powder box.
- Smooth or cover all sharp edges with tape.

To Use
- Children turn the top of the powder container to close the holes in the opening.
- They turn the box upside down and then fill it with water.
- Then they turn the top of the container to open the top and allow water to sprinkle through the holes.

Box Sifter

 Boxes

Materials
ice cream carton
ice pick (adults only)

To Make
- Away from the children, use the ice pick to punch holes into the bottom of the ice cream carton.

To Use
- Children fill the carton with sand and allow the sand to sift through the holes in the carton.

Milk Carton Boat

 Boxes

Materials
half-gallon milk carton
tape
craft knife (adults only)
construction paper
scissors
craft stick

To Make
- Place a half-gallon milk carton on its side.
- Tape the opening securely closed.
- Away from the children, use a craft knife to make a cut down the middle of the carton, leaving the bottom intact.
- Fold the boat open.
- Cut out a large sail from construction paper and tape it onto a craft stick.
- Tape the craft stick to the back of the boat.

To Use
- Children place the boat in the water table.

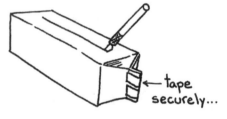

tape securely...

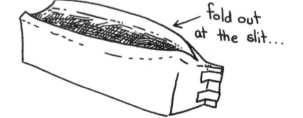

fold out at the slit...

Sockdozer

Socks/Pantyhose

Materials
sock
sand

To Make
- Fill a tube sock with sand.
- Tie the opening securely closed.

To Use
- Children drag or push the "sockdozer" through sand to make roads.

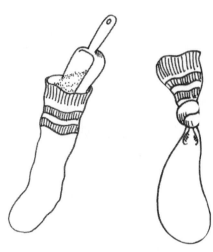

Bottles

Miscellaneous

Materials
different sizes of plastic bottles
scissors
craft knife (adults only)
duct tape

To Make
- Away from the children, use scissors and a craft knife to cut off the tops of a variety of different sizes of plastic bottles. Tape the edges of the bottles if they are sharp.

To Use
- Children use the tops of bottles as funnels and the bottoms of bottles as containers for pouring and measuring water or sand.

Music and Movement

Worm Bag

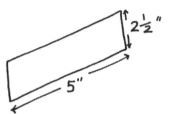

Bags

Materials

construction paper in a variety of colors
scissors
animal stickers
markers
paper lunch bag

To Make

- Cut out 30 strips, 2 ½" x 5", from colored construction paper.
- Put animal stickers on the bottoms of 26 of the paper strips.
- On the bottoms of the other four strips, use a marker to draw a picture of a worm.
- Decorate a lunch bag with silly, cartoon-style worms.
- Put the paper strips into the decorated bag and shake the bag to mix up the strips.

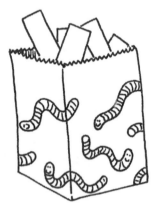

To Use

- Gather the children into a circle.
- Pass the bag to the first child in the circle.
- The child pulls out a strip from the bag and identifies the animal on it.
- If a worm is on the strip, the child yells, "Wiggle Worms!" and everyone stands up and then wiggles back in place in the circle.
- Continue passing the worm bag around the circle until all the children have had a turn or until all the strips have been pulled out.
- Collect the strips and play again if the children are interested.

Paper Bag Maracas

 Bags

Materials
paper lunch bags
brightly colored paint
paintbrushes
dry beans
tape
yarn

To Make
- Double the paper bags by putting one bag inside the other.
- Decorate the bags using bright colors of paint.
- When the paint is dry, fill the bags with ½ cup of dry beans.
- Tape the opening securely closed. Then tie it with yarn.

To Use
- Children shake the bags to music.

Ice Cream Box Shaker

 Boxes

Materials
clean, empty half-gallon ice cream carton with a lid
noise-making materials, such as dried beans, rice, popcorn kernels, pebbles, jingle bells, or paper clips
tape

To Make

- Place a variety of materials that make noise inside the ice cream carton.
- Tape the lid onto the carton using several layers of tape.

To Use

- Children shake the box to make music.

Shaker Boxes

 Boxes

Materials

small gift boxes with lids

tape

materials that make noise, such as dried beans, rice, pebbles, bottle caps, paper clips, or jingle bells

To Make

- Fill each box with a different noise-producing material.
- Tape the lids onto the boxes using several layers of tape.

To Use

- Children shake the boxes to make different rhythmic sounds.

Bongo Drums

 Boxes

Materials

glue

3 round oatmeal containers

duct tape

To Make

- Glue the lids onto the oatmeal containers.
- Use duct tape to fasten the three containers together in a triangle or in a straight line.

glue lid on securely...

OATMEAL

GLUE

To Use

- Children tap on the tops of the containers to make rhythms.

Milk Carton Guitar

 Boxes

Materials
clean, empty half-gallon milk carton
tape
craft knife (adults only)
4 large rubber bands

To Make

- Rinse and dry the milk carton.
- Tape the top closed.
- Away from the children, use a craft knife to cut out a rectangle in one side.
- Wrap four large rubber bands around the carton.

To Use

- Children use their fingers to strum across the rubber bands to make musical sounds.

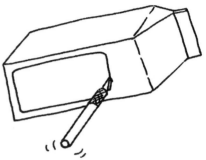

Sandpaper Musical Instruments

 Boxes

Materials

small- or medium-size cardboard boxes
craft knife (adults only)
coarse sandpaper
scissors
glue
duct tape
elastic

To Make

- Away from the children, use a craft knife to cut out 4" squares from the boxes.
- Cut sandpaper into squares a little smaller than 4".
- Glue the sandpaper squares onto one side of each cardboard square.
- Tape strips of elastic to the backs of the squares (the side without the sandpaper) so that the children can slip their hands under the elastic and hold the squares.

To Use

- Children put their hands through the squares and rub them together to keep time to music.

Obstacle Course

 Boxes

Materials

riding toys
balls
boxes
blocks
mats or cushions
stopwatch

To Make

- This activity can be quickly arranged and works well for inclement weather days.
- Talk with the children about what an obstacle course is.
- Arrange a variety of objects, such as riding toys, balls, boxes, and blocks, in such a way that children can complete the course with some effort. Place mats or cushions in areas where children may fall.

To Use

- Encourage the children to complete the course as quickly as possible.
- Introduce the idea of using a stopwatch to time the children's efforts. Encourage the children to compete against their own best time.

Box Maze

 Boxes

Materials

large- and medium-size boxes
duct tape
craft knife (adults only)

To Make

- Remove any staples and cover any rough edges of the boxes with duct tape.
- Away from the children, use a craft knife to cut doors and windows into the sides of the boxes. Include enough door and windows to allow for adequate supervision.
- Join the boxes together with duct tape. Make turns and forks, so the maze will be interesting.

To Use

- Children explore moving through the maze.
- Separate the boxes and join them together in a different way to add interest.

Glove Bells

 Gloves/Mittens

Materials

gloves
jingle bells
needle and thread (adults only)

To Make

- Sew jingle bells securely onto each finger of the gloves.

To Use

- Children wear one or two gloves and shake their hands to make music.

Outside

Paper Bag Kickball

 Bags

Materials

medium-size paper bag
newspapers
stapler
duct tape

To Make

- Stuff the bag with crumpled newspapers until it is about ¾ full.
- Mold the bag to make it as round as possible.
- Fold over the top of the bag and staple it closed.
- Cover the stapled section with duct tape.

To Use

- Children kick the bag, toss it to a friend, or throw it into a box.

Bag Kites

Bags

Materials

large paper bag
scissors
tape
colored ribbons

To Make

- Cut off the bottom of the bag.
- Cut out a 3" wide strip from the piece of cut-off bag bottom.
- Tape the strip across the opening of the bag to make a handle.
- Tape colored ribbons to the opposite end of the bag.

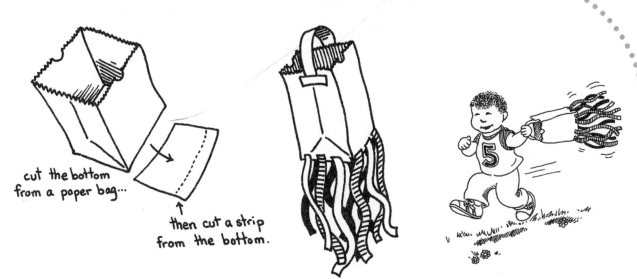

cut the bottom from a paper bag...

then cut a strip from the bottom.

To Use
- Children hold the bag handle and run with the bag to make the "kite" flutter.

Stack and Fall

Boxes

Materials
colored contact paper
scissors
10 empty salt boxes
3 beanbags

To Make
- Cut contact paper to fit around the salt boxes.
- Remove the adhesive from the contact paper and cover the salt boxes.

To Use
- Children stack the boxes any way they choose and then attempt to knock them over with beanbags or a paper bag ball (see page 152). (Pantyhose balls are too light to use for this activity.)

Piñata Box

 Boxes

Materials
cardboard box
confetti
tape
colored tissue paper
glue
crepe paper streamers
plastic bat

To Make
- Place confetti inside the box.
- Tape the opening securely closed.
- Glue colored tissue paper and crepe paper streamers over the entire box.

To Use
- Hang the box from a tree or play structure.
- The children take turns hitting the box with a plastic bat. Make sure the other children stand back while the child is hitting the box.
- The goal is for a child to open the box and let confetti shower over the children.

Tunnels

 Boxes

Materials
several large appliance boxes
duct tape
craft knife (adults only)

To Make

- Check the boxes for staples or other sharp edges. Remove all staples and cover any sharp edges with duct tape to make the boxes safe.
- Away from the children, use a craft knife cut off the tops and bottoms of the boxes.
- Cut out large holes in the sides of the boxes. Make some holes large enough for a child to put his or her body through, and make other holes just large enough to peek through.
- Tape the boxes together, end-to-end to make a tunnel.

To Use

- Children crawl through the tunnel, peeking out the holes along the way.

Parade Prop Box

 Boxes

Materials

copy paper box
parade props, such as crepe paper streamers, ribbons, paper hats, or party horns
marker
paper and pen
tape
portable cassette player and parade music

To Make

- Place all the parade items inside a copy paper box with a lid.
- Use a marker to label the box "Parade."
- On a sheet of paper, make a list of all the items contained in the box.
- Tape the list to the inside of the lid.

To Use

- Children use the materials in the box to decorate the riding toys.
- Play parade music as the children ride the decorated toys around the playground.

Car Wash

 Boxes

Materials

large cardboard box, such as a refrigerator box
craft knife (adults only)
tape
crepe paper streamers
riding toys

To Make

- Away from the children, use a craft knife to cut off both ends of a large cardboard box.
- Reinforce the box by wrapping tape around the sides of the box.
- In the center of one of the openings, tape crepe paper streamers along the top of the box.

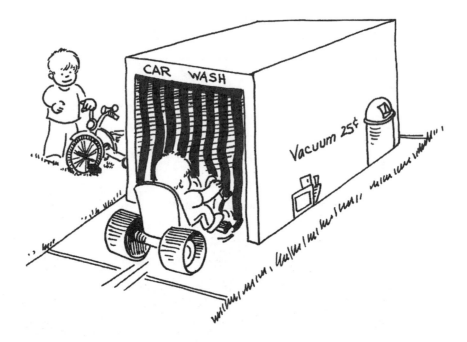

To Use

- Children ride the riding toys through the box to get a pretend car wash.

Fill 'er Up

 Boxes

Materials

medium-size cardboard box
craft knife (adults only)
old garden hose
tape
grip nozzle
markers
riding toys

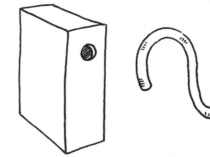

To Make

- Away from the children, use a craft knife to cut out a small hole in one side of the box (near the top).
- Cut off 3' from an old garden hose.
- Insert the cut end of the garden hose into the hole in the box and securely tape it in place.
- Attach a grip nozzle to the other end of the hose.
- Use markers to add details to make the box look like a gas pump.

To Use

- Children use the gas pump to "fill up" the riding toys as they play.

Windsock

 Boxes

Materials

oatmeal container
craft knife (adults only)
construction paper
scissors
glue
hole punch
string
crepe paper streamers
tape

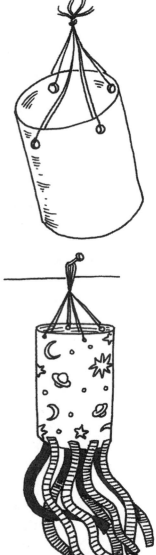

To Make

- Away from the children, use a craft knife to cut off the bottom and top of the oatmeal container.
- Cut a piece of construction paper to fit around the container. Cover the container with the construction paper and glue it in place.
- Use a hole punch to make four holes evenly spaced around the rim of one end of the container.
- Thread string through the holes and tie the ends together to make a hanger.
- Tape crepe paper streamers around the opposite end of the container.

To Use

- Hang the windsock outside so the children can observe how the wind makes the streamers move.

Mitten Horseshoes

 Gloves/Mittens

Materials
several mittens
dry beans
needle/thread
hula hoops

To Make
- Fill mittens with dry beans and sew the opening securely closed.
- Place hula hoops about 10' apart.

To Use
- Children take turns standing in one hula hoop and tossing the mittens into the next hula hoop.
- Use hula hoops for many different activities, including grouping and sorting.

Pantyhose Balls

 Socks/Pantyhose

Materials
pantyhose
scissors
fiberfill

To Make
- Cut off the legs of pantyhose. Cut the pantyhose into 12" lengths.
- Tie a knot in one open end of the hose and turn it inside out, putting the knot on the inside.
- Fill the hose with fiberfill and shape it into a ball.
- Tie a knot to close the opening.
- Turn the panty portion of the pantyhose inside out and knot the leg openings securely closed.

- Turn the panty portion right side out and stuff with fiberfill.
- Tie the opening securely closed.

To Use

- These soft balls are great for throwing. They are easy to wash and dry and fun to use for tossing games.
- The large pantyhose ball is fun for beginning "catching" activities, tossing into a basket or box, or throwing through a hoop.

Pantyhose Bats

 Socks/Pantyhose

Materials
wire clothes hangers
duct tape
pantyhose
scissors

To Make

- Bend the wire coat hangers into a baseball bat shape.
- Twist the hook portions into a tight handle.
- Wrap layers of duct tape around the handles to cover any sharp edges.
- Cut off one leg from a pair of pantyhose.
- Stretch a pantyhose leg over each wire shape and secure leftover hose with duct tape around the handle.

To Use

- Children use the bats with pantyhose balls for playing alone or with a friend.

Toss and Catch

 Socks/Pantyhose

Materials

pantyhose
scissors
fiberfill
craft knife (adults only)
large plastic jug with a handle
tape
yarn

use a craft knife to remove bottom of a plastic jug.

To Make

- Cut off the leg from a pair of pantyhose and cut it into a 12" length.
- Tie a knot in one open end of the hose and turn it inside out, putting the knot on the inside.
- Fill the hose with fiberfill, shape it into a ball, and tie a knot to close the opening.
- Away from the children, use a craft knife to cut off the bottom of a large plastic jug with a handle.
- Smooth or cover all sharp edges with tape.
- Tie a piece of yarn to the pantyhose ball and tape the other end of the yarn to the inside of the jug.

To Use

- Children hold the jug by the handle, swing the ball up in the air, and catch it in the jug.

Dear Parents,

We need your help to create wonderful toys. Please send any of the materials that are checked. All materials should be thoroughly clean and dry.

Thank you!

- ☐ Aluminum foil or wax paper boxes
- ☐ Animal stickers
- ☐ Band-Aids, assorted sizes
- ☐ Baskets
- ☐ Blocks
- ☐ Bottle caps and lids
- ☐ Bubble wrap
- ☐ Butcher paper
- ☐ Buttons
- ☐ Cardboard boxes
- ☐ Cardboard tubes
- ☐ Cereal boxes
- ☐ Chalk
- ☐ Clay
- ☐ Coffee cans
- ☐ Construction paper
- ☐ Contact paper, clear or patterned
- ☐ Cotton gloves
- ☐ Craft feathers
- ☐ Craft foam
- ☐ Craft sticks
- ☐ Crepe paper streamers
- ☐ Duct tape
- ☐ Fabric
- ☐ Fabric glue
- ☐ Fabric paint
- ☐ Felt
- ☐ Gardening gloves
- ☐ Gloves, all sizes

- ☐ Glue
- ☐ Greeting cards, used
- ☐ Hair gel
- ☐ Half-gallon ice cream carton, with lid
- ☐ Hula hoops
- ☐ Index cards
- ☐ Jar and juice can lids
- ☐ Jingle bells
- ☐ Lace
- ☐ Large matchboxes (sliding type)
- ☐ Magazines
- ☐ Magnets
- ☐ Marbles
- ☐ Markers
- ☐ Masking tape
- ☐ Mesh produce bags
- ☐ Milk cartons, assorted sizes
- ☐ Mittens, all sizes
- ☐ Newspaper
- ☐ Oatmeal containers
- ☐ Paint
- ☐ Paintbrushes
- ☐ Pantyhose
- ☐ Paper cups
- ☐ Paper grocery bags
- ☐ Paper lunch bags
- ☐ Paper plates
- ☐ Permanent markers

- ☐ Pie tins
- ☐ Ping-Pong balls
- ☐ Pipe cleaners
- ☐ Plastic bags, all sizes
- ☐ Plastic bottles and jars
- ☐ Playdough
- ☐ Pompoms
- ☐ Popsicle sticks
- ☐ Potato chip cans
- ☐ Ribbon
- ☐ Sequins
- ☐ Shoeboxes, with and without lids
- ☐ Socks, all sizes
- ☐ Sponges
- ☐ Staplers
- ☐ Straws, drinking
- ☐ Tempera paint
- ☐ Tissue boxes
- ☐ Tissue paper
- ☐ Tongue depressors
- ☐ Tube socks, all sizes
- ☐ Tweezers
- ☐ Twine
- ☐ Velcro
- ☐ Watercolors
- ☐ Wiggle eyes
- ☐ Wire clothes hangers
- ☐ Wrapping paper
- ☐ Yarn

*Publisher permits unlimited photocopying for personal use.

Index